The Miracle of Navajo Technical University

A unique institution of higher learning integrating trades education with academic learning, rigorous research, and economic development

Thomas (Tom) Davis
Dale Morgan
Harold (Scott) Halliday
Sheena Begay and staff
Jared Ribble
Thiagarajan Soundappan
Al Kuslikis

Navajo Technical University Press
Crownpoint, NM

The Miracle of Navajo Technical University

THE MIRACLE OF NAVAJO TECHNICAL UNIVERSITY

Navajo Technical University/Navajo Technical University Press
Mailing Address: Navajo Technical University, PO Box 849.
Crownpoint, NM 87313
www.navajotech.edu.

Navajo Technical University/ Navajo Technical University, Tom Davis
-- 1st ed.
ISBN 978-1-964157-03-0

Cover design by Ethel Mortenson Davis
Cover photos, top right, NTU graduation ceremony taken by NTU marketing staff, bottom left, Adriane Tenequer working in the Center for Advanced Manufacturing, and bottom left, Dr. Elmer Guy at an American Indian Higher Education Conference taken by NTU marketing staff.

To Raymond Redhouse,
Teacher
Medicine Man
Crystal Holder
Who blessed buildings, ceremonies,
and celebrations at NTU
for decades

*"Go and tell the Navajo people that education
is the ladder."*

—CHIEF MANUELITO

Acknowledgements

Parts of this book appeared in the *Navajo Technical University Annual Report, 2025*. Crownpoint, New Mexico: Navajo Technical University, January 2025.

Davis, Thomas. "How to Not Fall Off the Stage During Commencement," *Meditations on Ceremonies of Beginnings*. Durango, Colorado: Tribal College Press, 2020.

About Navajo Technical University Press

The Press was initiated by Gene Hult at the Chinle, Arizona Campus who worked with students to publish *Turquoise*, a student anthology of creative writing. The Press is dedicated to publishing student work as well as scholarly books about topics of interest to the TCU community.

Board of Regents

Contents

Acknowledgements 7

About Navajo Technical University Press 7

Board of Regents 7

Introduction.. 13

A Short History of Navajo Technical University................ 17

Beginnings 17

The Beginning of the Tribal College University
Movement 20

Navajo Technical University's Historical Development . 21

Navajo Technical University Today............................... 22

Campuses and Instructional Sites............................... 24

Partnerships and Collaborations................................. 26

The World Indigenous Nations Higher Education
Consortium 27

Summary 28

Elmer Guy, Visionary President of the University 29

The Extraordinary NTU Educational Model 85

Building a Research University...................................... 86

The Center for Advanced Manufacturing 87

The NTU Veterinary Hospital and Educational Programs
.... 88

Other Research/Educational Projects........................... 89

The NSF Nexus Prize 90

Supporting Students 91

Competitions 91

E-Learning at NTU 93

Technology Infrastructure at NTU 95

Projects Supporting the Navajo Nation 100

Business, Entrepreneurial Culture, and Creativity 101

Navajo Technical University Innovation Center 103

The Hole in Economic Development Efforts by
Universities in the United States 103

The Development of Iíná LLC 104

Capstone Courses 106

Summary of the NTU Higher Education Model 107

Graphic Environmental Model Components 109

Relationships and Interactions 111

Graphic Representation of Outline 112

Summary 112

The Future 115

Navajo Technical University Statistics 131

Portraits of NTU Graduates 147

Dwight Carlson 148

Jared Ribble 151

Jacqueline Lee 154

Marcie Vandever... 157

Hansen Tapaha 160

Twila Largo.. 163

Warlance Chee.. 166

Terri Ami 168

Wayant Billey 171

Daylana Hanna... 173

Robinson Tom 175

Sheena Begay... 177

Leadership at NTU 181

Provost, Dr. Colleen W. Bowman 181

Vice President of Operations, Jason Arviso 184

Prospectus for the Long and Short-term Development of Iíná, the Holding Company 187

Prospectus for Navajo Advanced Manufacturing Enterprises... 189

Navajo Advanced Manufacturing Enterprises (NAME) Abstract 189

Overall Marketing Prospectus 191

Initial Marketing Approach for Each Division.............. 195

Metal AM Powder Manufacturing and Characterization 195

Metal AM Printing 195

Injection Molding and Machining............................ 196

Sandia National Laboratory Electronics Calibration Center 197

Initial Equipment and Instrumentation to Be Installed, Phase 1 197

Metal AM Printing 197

Other Equipment to be Utilized in Phase 1................. 198

Market Prospectus: Powder Manufacturingfor Metal AM, First Development of NAME 199

Metal AM Powder Manufacturing and Characterization 199

Customer Base 200

Navajo Advanced Manufacturing Enterprise's Placement in the Market 201

Key Initial Benchmarks 202

History of and Plans for a Navajo Medical School 203

Historical Efforts to Create a Medical School for the Navajo Nation 205

The Current Proposal for NTU to Create a Medical School 206

Chemistry and the NEST Lab 215

Artificial Intelligence (AI) at NTU 219

ABOUT 240

THE AUTHORS 240

Notes 247

Introduction

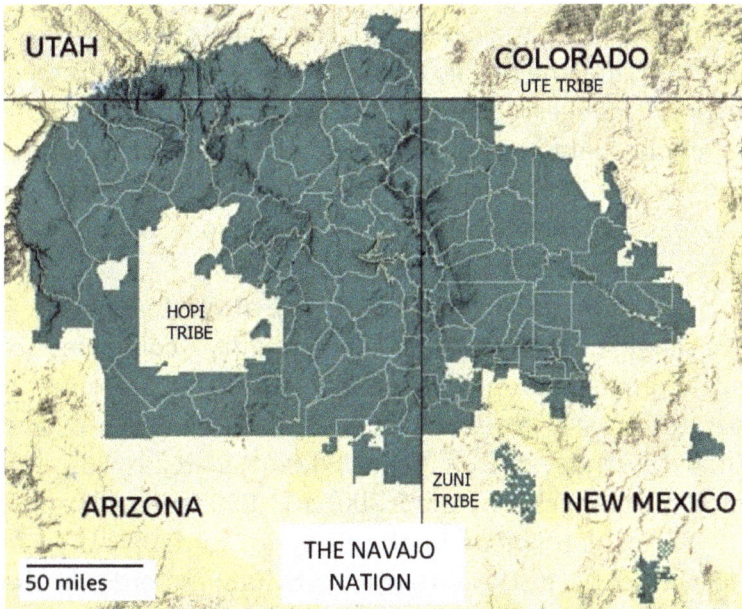

UTAH · COLORADO · UTE TRIBE · HOPI TRIBE · ZUNI TRIBE · ARIZONA · NEW MEXICO · THE NAVAJO NATION · 50 miles

The Navajo, or Diné, people have lived in one of the most poverty-stricken areas of the United States for a long time. After the Long Walk, which was forced after the U.S. Army under Kit Carson defeated the last of Navajo resistance against an American invasion, the Diné never recovered the well-being that had characterized their civilization stretching back thousands of years.

On the Long Walk, where the Navajo people were forced to march from their homes in what is now Arizona and New Mexico to Bosque Redondo and Fort Sumner in New Mexico in 1864, many people died or were captured for servitude to non-Indian families. When crops failed in Fort Sumner and starvation became a plague seemingly without end, the U.S. government finally relented and let the Diné return to their homelands, but they came home without resources and had to live in a country based upon land ownership, competition between individuals and business, and a dollar economy, all ideas alien to their traditional culture.

Over time, the Navajo have made progress in addressing their challenges. The Nation today has reduced both unemployment and poverty rates from historical highs, and the number of people with high school diplomas or college degrees have increased, but it remains one of the most impoverished regions in the United States.

The Nation itself is roughly the size of West Virginia. It is the largest Reservation in the country, comprised of approximately 16 million acres or 25,000 square miles. It has territory in three states: Arizona, New Mexico, and Utah. Mostly located on the high desert, plateaus, hills, and mountain ranges are from 5,000 to 11,000 feet in altitude.

Official enrollment in the Tribe is currently 399,494 individuals. Many Navajo live in communities bordering the Nation or in cities well off the Reservation such as Albuquerque, NM and Phoenix, AZ. On the Reservation itself, the current population is approximately 147,000 people, although that can fluctuate depending on economic conditions in the rest of the country. When the labor market shrinks in places like Phoenix or Albuquerque, Navajos are often the first to be laid off. Then many families head back home.

Currently (February 2025) the Navajo Nation is reporting an unemployment rate of 48.5%. Limited employment opportunities are available on the reservation, and household incomes are low, reducing the amount of retail, wholesale, or other economic activity that can drive job creation. The average household income is reported at $8,240, well below federal poverty guidelines.

Substandard housing, poor health outcomes, elevated rates of crime, substance abuse, suicide, and other socio-economic conditions associated with other communities that have experienced systemic generational poverty are found throughout Navajo. In large parts of the reservation, households collect water from wells or population centers where running water is available in a variety of containers and then haul it to homes so families can have the water to drink, wash dishes, take baths, or keep their homes clean. There are also areas without Internet access or even access to electricity or telephone services.

The miracle of Navajo Technical University is that its campuses and instructional sites are in isolated, small communities that have, like the rest of Navajo, experienced generational poverty. Still, it is has become internationally recognized as one of the most important institutions of minority higher education in the United States.

Chartered by the Navajo Nation and largely funded through federal resources (although the Navajo Nation, the states of New Mexico and Arizona, and private foundations have also made significant investments), it is laying the foundation, along with its sister Navajo chartered college, Diné College, for a more independent and prosperous Navajo future, providing a model for how governments around the world can go about moving toward solving one of the world's grand challenges, the complex set of issues negatively impacting a geographic region's economy and people's health, education, and access to basic services.

Admittedly, Navajo Tech's accomplishments, although impressive, are a long way from accomplishing what needs to be done before it is declared the solution to the grand challenge of poverty. Grand Challenges are a family of initiatives designed to foster innovation to solve key global health and development problems. Even though Navajo Tech is still developing as a model designed to demonstrate how to reverse the forces that create generational poverty, the university's accomplishments to date, as they are described in this book, are as powerful an argument for continued investment in the nation's tribal colleges and universities as can be made.

CHAPTER 1

A Short History of Navajo Technical University

Navajo Technical University (NTU), chartered by the Navajo Nation under the auspices of the Tribally Controlled Colleges and Universities Assistance Act of 1978 (25 U.S.C)., located in the high desert of New Mexico and Arizona, has created one of the most extraordinary stories of higher education innovation in the United States.

Beginnings

A workforce development program that became a tribal college and then a tribal university, NTU, as it's often referred to by the Navajo, or Diné, people, started out at as the Navajo Skills Center in 1969. Few people living on the Navajo Reservation had jobs in 1969. The unemployment rate on Navajo during that period was 62.1% of the workforce.[1]

At that point, the Navajo Reservation was one of the largest pockets of deep poverty in the United States, a circumstance that had existed since the return of the Diné to their homelands after the devastation of the Long Walk where the entire tribe was marched at gunpoint to Bosque Redondo and Fort Sumner in eastern New Mexico. Thousands of people died during multiple, torturous 18-day journeys. The Long Walk was followed by disaster when crops repeatedly failed, causing widespread starvation, and water and even firewood was too limited for the Navajo and Mescalero Apache forcibly interned there. The Navajo returned to their homelands in Northern New Mexico and Arizona and Southern Utah after the Treaty of Bosque Redondo was negotiated and signed on June 1, 1868.

Navajo Skills Center was set up through a grant from the federal government in Washington DC to provide what today is known as workforce training with the hope that, by providing vocational/technical training, the unemployment rate could be reduced and some of the widespread poverty could be at least partially alleviated.

The Navajo legislature and President appointed a Diné board to oversee education activities at the center under the Navajo Division of Labor. The headquarters for the center was then established in some old, abandoned buildings in Crownpoint, New Mexico, although the expectation was that the center would serve all Diné people. The original curriculum emphasized skills like carpentry, electrical trades, and secretarial science, all of which exist as courses of study at NTU today in one form or another.

Peter McDonald was the Chairman of the Navajo Nation when the Navajo Skills Center was established. He described his memory of the founding of the Center in a text to President Elmer Guy:

In the 1970s when we were fighting the unions for not hiring Navajos because our workers were not union members, I got $3 million dollars from the U.S. Department of Labor to establish a Manpower Center in Crownpoint. There was an old dirt airstrip; we had the Chapter and BIA move the air strip west to part of Art Arviso's land (present day airstrip). Thanks to Art.

We then leveled the old dirt runway and built a Manpower Center to train our people in all the major skill areas and forced the U.S. Department of Labor to force the union to accept our trained workers into the union without probation or waiting.

Some of the present-day buildings in use by the NTU were Manpower buildings. Later, it was natural to create a Junior College and thus the present day, the best Technical University this side of MIT. Past leaders of Crownpoint are to be commended for their vision and cooperation with the tribe.

2

The significance of the decision to locate the center at Crownpoint lies in its location in sight of Mount Taylor, or, in Navajo, *Tsoodził*, which translates to Turquois Mountain. *Tsoodził* is one of four sacred mountains to the Navajo, the southern-most mountain. The other sacred mountains are:

Blanca Peak (east) *Sisnaajiní*
San Francisco Peaks (west) *Doko'oosłííd*
and Hesperus Peak (north) *Dibéntsaa*

During the return of the Diné people after leaving Fort Sumner, they saw *Tsoodził* in the distance. This gave them not only a feeling of hope but also let them know they were getting close to their homelands.

The Beginning of the Tribal College Movement

In 1966, a group of visionary Navajo and the Superintendent of the School District, Robert Roessel Jr., founded the Rough Rock Demonstration School in Rough Rock, Arizona, which started the journey toward the tribal colleges and universities movement chartered by tribes throughout the United States. The idea behind the Demonstration School was that by emphasizing Navajo culture, history, and language, and trying to reverse the direction of American Indian education initiated with the start of the boarding and religious school era at Carlisle Indian School in Pennsylvania in 1869, the widespread failure of young Native students to succeed in education could be reversed. By emphasizing the strength of Navajo culture, language, the entire history of the tribal people being served by the school, and even the spirituality of the tribe, the founders of Rough Rock reasoned, young students would discard feelings of inferiority and frustration typically experienced in state and BIA operated schools and embrace the knowledge and skills education had to offer.

The Rough Rock experiment, largely discounted by both the federal government and many mainstream educators, quickly evolved into two movements, the tribal college and Indian controlled schools movements.[3] The tribal college movement started when the leaders of the demonstration school, including Robert and his wife Ruth Roessel and others like Dillon Platero, decided that what was being accomplished for young students at Rough Rock would be equally effective and powerful at the community college level. Working again with the tribal legislature and President, Navajo Community College was established and eventually permanently located in Tsaile, Arizona.

In 1972, the founding of the American Indian Higher Education Consortium (AIHEC) by six colleges that had little or no funding[4] launched the tribal college movement in the United States. With American Indian leaders increasingly aware of under-educated populations, the ideas driving Navajo Community College seemed to potentially contain a long-term answer to at least some of the problems Native peoples were facing through lack of access to higher education. Mainstream institutions of higher learning had largely failed to graduate significant numbers of Native students.

Navajo Technical University's Historical Development

As the tribal colleges and universities (TCU) movement got underway, the incipient college in Crownpoint was starting to evolve from its workforce development roots, maintaining those roots but looking toward a larger role in Diné education. In 1984, the Navajo Skills Center was accredited by the North Central Association of Colleges and Schools with a specialty school accreditation. In 1985, the Board of Directors changed the center's name to the Crownpoint Institute of Technology (CIT). The idea was to develop beyond the certificates, which had up to that time been the most advanced credential a student could earn, to technical (Associate of Applied Science, AAS) degrees.

Along with other TCU members of AIHEC, CIT became a land grant college in 1994. In February of 2006, CIT first achieved initial accreditation as a full-fledged community college from the North Central Association of Colleges and Schools. Shortly after that was achieved, CIT was renamed Navajo Technical College. In 2007, the first of its instructional sites away from Crownpoint was established in Chinle, AZ. Then in 2010 three baccalaureate degrees, Information Technology, Digital Manufacturing, and New Media, became accredited. This accomplishment was followed up by the accreditation of NTU's first master's degree in Diné Language, Culture, and Leadership in 2013. That same year the Navajo legislature and President passed legislation changing the college's name to Navajo Technical University. In 2023, the university became a PhD granting institution when the Higher Learning Commission approved a Doctor of Philosophy degree in Navajo Culture and Language Sustainability, the first doctoral degree offered by any of the U.S.'s thirty-four TCUs.

Navajo Technical University Today

This history is only the start of NTU's remarkable development as an innovative institution of higher learning, however. Today the university offers an extraordinary career ladder of micro-credentials, certificates, and associate, baccalaureate, master, and PhD degree programs. A student that earns a micro-credential in carpentry can then earn a certificate in electrical trades, then go on to earn a baccalaureate degree in Electrical Engineering and then go from there into the master degree program in Electrical Engineering. NTU is currently preparing to launch a doctorate in Electrical Engineering in 2026.

Most of the curriculum at NTU is either centered in trade programs like Culinary Arts, Baking, Construction Technology, Automotive Technology, Welding, Plumbing, or Energy Systems, or in Science, Technology, Engineering, Math (STEM), or health degrees, although it also offers degrees in areas like Early Childhood Education, Law

Advocate, Criminal Justice, Veterinary Technology, and Creative Writing and New Media. These are mostly degrees that the Navajo Nation has had interest in seeing developed over the years of NTU's existence.

In addition to accreditation from the Higher Learning Commission, NTU also offers specialty credentialing or accreditation in areas like Culinary Arts, Baking, and the construction trades as well as ABET accreditation[5] for Electrical Engineering (B.S.), Industrial Engineering (B.S.), Information Technology (B.A.S.), Advanced Manufacturing Engineering Technology (B.A.S.), Chemical Engineering Technology (A.A.S.), and Engineering Technology (A.A.S.). Currently it is the only ABET accredited TCU.

The university is also the largest tribal university in the United States, serving mostly Navajo students but also students from other tribes, especially the Zuni Nation, as well as from other communities.

NTU lives by the Din Philosophy of Education, or DPE. DPE is drawn from the traditional culture described in the teachings given to the Navajo, Diné, people. NTU's Mission Statement says that the University is committed to a high quality, student-oriented, hands-on learning environment based on the Diné cultural principles: Nitsáhákees (Thinking), Nahat'á (Planning), Iiná (Living), and Sihasin (Assurance).

Campuses and Instructional Sites

Overview of the Main Campus in Crownpoint

The main NTU campus is in Crownpoint, NM, a small unincorporated community in the checkerboarded part of the Navajo Nation.[6] In addition to the campus, the community has a chapterhouse, tribal government buildings, tribal police offices, and other government facilities. The Crownpoint campus offers the most majors and degrees of any of the sites and is where the graduate degree programs are centered.

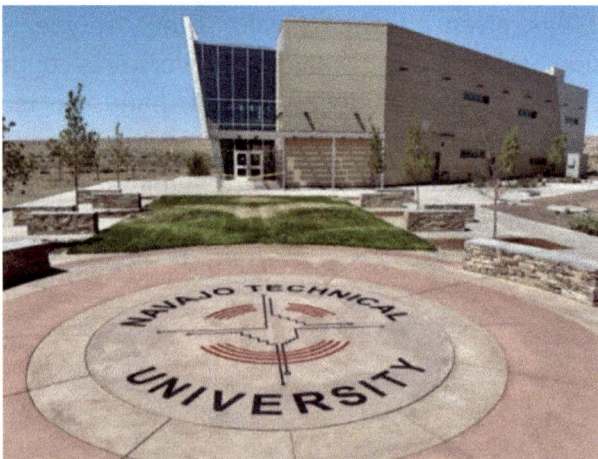

Chinle Campus

The first instructional site opened by NTU was in Chinle, AZ close to the geographic center of the Navajo Nation. Chinle is at the mouth of the famous Canyon de Chelly National Monument and has a tourism economy that supports more than 500 jobs in the area. In addition to chapter house offices, Chinle has several restaurants and hotels and a retail sector. The Chinle site does not have as many degree offerings as Crownpoint, but the number of degrees it has been offering has been steadily expanding.

Later, the instructional site at Teec Nos Pos, AZ, close to the four corners where Arizona, New Mexico, Utah, and Colorado borders meet, was opened. The smallest instructional site, it is also in one of the smaller Navajo communities, not far from the Ute Nation in Colorado. Only general education courses and vocational degrees are offered at this site.

Following the opening of Teec Nos Pos, the Bond Wilson instructional site was opened in partnership with North Central Consolidated School District in Kirtland, NM. Dedicated to vocational/technical education, it only offers a few courses of study and associate of applied science degree programs, although those have been expanding.

The last instructional site was created after the University of New Mexico—Gallup abandoned its higher education efforts on the Zuni Nation. The Zuni, a Pueblo people, then asked NTU if it would partner with its Nation to keep the A:shiwi College & Career Readiness Center open and to mentor their efforts to establish A:shiwi as a tribal college. Several NTU degrees are offered at the A:shiwi instructional site as the Zuni people work to create their own TCU.

Partnerships and Collaborations

As Navajo Tech evolved into a university, it developed an increasing number of partnerships and collaborations. The early examples were almost all developed in concert with AIHEC and its tribal college membership or through its land grant status. The circle of partnerships expanded when CIT expanded its work with AIHEC, the National Association for Equal Opportunity in Higher Education (NAFEO), and the Hispanic Association of Colleges and Universities (HACU) in implementing the Advanced Networking for Minority Serving Institutions (ANMSI). A National Science Foundation (NSF) funded project, ANMSI worked with close to one hundred tribal, historically black, and Hispanic-serving colleges and universities to improve technology infrastructure and establish a community of practice in technology operations and maintenance.

As CIT became NTC and then NTU, collaborations with colleges like Salish Kootenai College in Montana, Bay Mills Community College in Northern Michigan, Southwest Indian Polytechnic Institute (SIPI) in Albuquerque, New Mexico, and Diné College in Tsaile, Arizona became increasingly common. Partnerships were usually anchored in STEM projects funded by different federal agencies or private foundations like the Kellogg or Gates Foundation, but sometimes opportunities were identified in other areas such as Student Support Services.

Today NTU has many partnerships and/or collaborations with universities such as Arizona State University, New Mexico Technical University, the University of New Mexico, Harvard University, the University of Kansas, and others. Higher education institutions across the U.S. often seek out Navajo Tech professors and administrators for such partnerships or collaborations because of the international reputation that has been developing over a long period of time.

In addition, several projects are underway with National Laboratories such as Sandia National Laboratory, Los Alamos National Laboratory, both in New Mexico, or Oak Ridge National Laboratory in Tennessee and an even larger number of private sector corporations in fields ranging from Advanced Manufacturing to Chemistry to Environmental Engineering on projects such as the creation of a new battery technology for Aerospace, energy storage, and the electric automobile industries.

The World Indigenous Nations Higher Education Consortium

One of the more significant developments in NTU's history has been its involvement in the World Indigenous Nations Higher Education Consortium (WINHEC). It was formed in Kananaskis, Canada, just before a World Indigenous Peoples' Conference on Education (WIPC) was held in 2002. Leaders of indigenous institutions of higher learning from the United States, including Tom Davis, who later became the Provost at NTU, and AIHEC Presidents like Lionel Bordeaux of Sinte Gleska University and Jim Shanley, President of Fort Peck Community College, and indigenous higher education leaders from New Zealand, Australia, Canada, Hawaii, the Sami in Europe, and Alaska were part of the work that occurred in Kananaskis. WINHEC has expanded the TCU model of indigenous controlled education to countries in Norway, Japan, Taiwan, South America, and the Asian continent.

Elmer Guy, the President of NTU, served as the Chairman of WINHEC for several years, and NTU has been involved throughout the organization's existence as it has established an international accreditation authority, an international university, developed important scholarly publications, become formally recognized by the United Nations, and championed indigenous teaching models.

CIT hosted WINHEC's annual gathering in Crownpoint at NTU in 2014. During this meeting, the World Indigenous Nations University was created. WINHEC continues to expand its reach across the globe with NTU as one of the core drivers of its development

Summary

Starting as a job training center on the Navajo Nation when the Navajo people had few resources at their disposal and an unemployment rate higher than almost anywhere else in the United States (few jobs existed for Diné adults or young people in even border communities like Gallup or Farmington in New Mexico or Holbrook, Arizona), NTU became a technical college, then a baccalaureate degree granting college, and then a full-fledged graduate degree granting and research university with a wide array of partnerships and collaborations. These exist with other major universities, national laboratories, and private sector firms located throughout the United States. Today NTU has both a national and international reputation as one of the most prestigious and innovative minority serving institutions of higher learning in the United States.

CHAPTER 2

Elmer Guy, Visionary President of the University

Dr. Elmer Guy has been one of the most consequential American Indian educational leaders in the United States since he became the President of the college that became NTU. Appointed to that position by the CIT Board of Directors in 2007, his leadership has not only created the largest tribally controlled university in the country but has also created a unique approach to tribal education that serves as a model for any indigenous institution of higher education in the world working to improve the economic and social well-being of their people. He has influenced the operations of other U.S. colleges and universities along the way. His vision of what a higher education institution can achieve has led to a tribal university that is not only creating benefits for the Navajo people but is also producing cutting edge work that has implications for societies throughout the world.

Dr. Guy's Parents

Dr. Guy was born in Sage Memorial Hospital located in Ganado, Arizona on the Navajo Reservation on January 23, 1954. His mother was taken to Ganado for the birth, a trip of just under 29 miles, since Chinle, where the family was living, only had a small medical clinic. Today the Chinle Indian Health Service hospital is in the geographic and population heart of the Navajo Nation.

Charles Kevin Guy Sr., Dr. Guy's father, was part of the Draper family that live around Del Muerto, AZ on the Navajo Nation. His grandparents were Notah and Elouise Draper. His father became a Guy, at least as he told the story to his five sons and five daughters, because his oldest sister was sent to boarding school.

The administrators there legally changed her name from Draper to Guy, saddling her three brothers and four sisters with the Guy name.

His mother, Ida Bia Guy, did not attend school beyond a Day School operated by the U.S. government, which just taught young children. She was an herbalist that often took her children to Canyon De Chelly, whose mouth is located near the outskirts of Chinle, to collect roots and plants to treat illnesses identified in traditional Navajo culture. To this day, Dr. Guy can identify many high desert plants on sight.

His mother was also steeped in Diné culture and ceremonies and made sure all her children were inculcated with the spiritual heritage of their people. She was especially good at getting the brothers and sisters to play string games designed to enhance memory and teach traditional songs sung in Navajo. Basically, according to Dr. Guy, she had a knack for making learning fun, which later served him well when he entered school.

Charles Guy worked at several jobs over his lifetime, bus driver for a Bureau of Indian Affair's school, worker for the road's department of the Reservation, and a maintenance and warehouse worker. During World War II he served as one of the famous Code Talkers who helped the U.S. Marines battle across the Pacific. He had volunteered for the Marines because he liked how their blue uniforms looked, but when the military found out he was fluent in Navajo, his Marine superiors sent him to school to learn the communication skills of a Code Talker. He served the United States until the end of the war and the Allied victory.

Early Life

As a child, Dr. Guy spent most of his time outdoors. Water had to be hauled from the well to the house, wood had to be chopped for the wood stove, and there were always animals that had to be herded, if they were sheep, or watered or fed. His dad always told him that you didn't really notice changes in weather if you were out in nature a lot. He said that you changed with nature when you spent a lot of time outside. The weather could get cold, but by then your body had adjusted to the cold.

After he got out of his toddler years, his father started getting him up at five a.m. every morning along with his brothers and sisters. His dad wanted to toughen his children up so that they could handle what was inevitably going to be a life filled with difficulties and setbacks, which was the common Navajo experience. He would take his young son outside in the early light before breakfast and have him start his day by running.

As he grew older, the distances he ran became longer and longer until Dr. Guy was going several miles a day on different routes in and around Chinle before he started his school day. None of his siblings wore gloves during the winter while they ran in the cold dark. There were also times when a policeman would stop them and shine a spotlight in their faces to see who they were, but they were always recognized and waved on their way.

Between his mother's ministrations with traditional medicines and treatments and his father's inculcation of physical discipline, none of the siblings had to visit the small Chinle Indian Health Services Clinic. Although Dr. Guy was small and wiry as he grew up (he was never tall enough to excel at basketball), he was always as healthy and energetic as any other boy at school.

The most powerful influence on his early life was not an unusual one for many young Navajo. His grandmother was especially careful about who among her grandchildren she would ask to take care of the sheep flock in the summers. He was excited when he and his favorite cousin were chosen. After getting the invitation from his grandparents, he then spent three summers watching over the sheep as they grazed in open fields near their house. This meant working with the sheep dogs and keeping watch to make sure that the flock was in good pasture and not threatened by coyotes or packs of wild dogs or other predators. The responsibility was huge, and he and his cousin were constantly questioned about their day or sometimes night when the sheep were grazing further afield.

Learning how to stay focused on what they were supposed to be doing and not getting distracted by the countless things that could have distracted the two of them while they were out on the high desert was difficult sometimes, but neither of them wanted to disappoint either the grandparents or their parents, so they learned how to meet the expectations placed upon them. Although there were times, Dr. Guy said, when the old saying, boys will be boys, had some resonance in their behavior, for the most part they grew into their responsibility and performed well.

Sheep herding ended when he finally grew old enough to get on the youth baseball teams that competed in the center of the Reservation. You could not be out every day with sheep if you also "had" to be at a baseball game halfway through the day. To a young Dr. Guy, baseball was important. He had gone out running early in the morning most of his life, and he was an athlete. That meant being a baseball player was important.

High School to the First Year of College

By the time he got into high school, Dr. Guy was already a good student. He had strong grades overall, and although not all his athletic dreams were working out quite the way he had imagined they would, he was still managing to play well enough in baseball to get on the junior varsity team. The challenge was that he was too short for basketball and a little too slight for football even though he was strong for his size. He'd chopped a lot of wood and hauled a lot of water.

A new teacher introduced wrestling to the high school when he was a sophomore, however, and his athletic fortunes turned. He didn't have to be bigger or taller in wrestling since wrestlers wrestled in their weight class. That meant he was competing against other high school boys roughly the same size he was.

During his sophomore year he wasn't at the top of the wrestling pyramid in the meets held around Northern Arizona where Chinle High School participated, but as he went into his junior year, he had become a force to be reckoned with, often being the only Chinle wrestler his age to win a series of matches meet after meet. His two older brothers had become state champions from the high school and kept telling him he could achieve that too. As a junior, he went to the Arizona state tournament. He did not end up in the championship match but placed fourth in state. Then, during his senior year, he was the runner-up at state after making a mistake in his state championship match.

He still remembers and regrets that mistake all these years later.

Academically, he continued being a good student in his classes and took the college preparatory classes available from the curriculum. The counselor at the high school met with him several times during his senior year and encouraged him to continue to college. Northern Arizona University in Flagstaff often accepted Navajo students from Chinle, and the counselor thought that would be a good place for him to apply. When he did apply, he was accepted and then enrolled with five other students from his graduating class.

The problem was that after he started classes in the fall, he wasn't sure what he was doing at the university. He didn't have a clear idea about what he wanted to go into for a career. He did not, frankly, know a lot of Navajo that had a professional career outside of a couple of teachers. The university environment and dorm life were different from what he was used to too. At home, he was immersed in Navajo life with his mother's belief in their culture and traditions all around him in the ceremonies and even conversations he had with his family and friends. He knew who he was. At Northern Arizona, everything was different.

He could handle the classwork, but he didn't feel like he belonged there. His non-Indian classmates were okay, but they knew where they were going for the most part and had a good idea about how they were going to get there. He felt mostly adrift and unsure about his future and where he was going to end up if he stayed where he was.

As the year wound to an end, he increasingly thought about his father's success as a Marine and a Code Talker. His dad never talked much about the war. The

Code Talkers had been sworn to secrecy and had agreed to never reveal what they had done to help win the war, but the way people around Chinle approached his dad made plain that he was held in high regard, partially because of his service in the Marine Corps. Thinking about all this, Dr. Guy decided that he would drop out of college and volunteer for the Marines. He could achieve at least some of the distinction his father had achieved.

When the year ended and he went home and told his mom and dad what he had decided, a storm broke out. His mother was especially opposed to his idea about joining the Marines. She was proud of what he had achieved by going to the university. Now he was turning his back on that.

As for the Marines, his dad and the Navajo who had served their country so well during the war had come back home, and not all the promises the government had made to them had been kept. They had helped the U.S. succeed at beating back the Japanese, but the government had not done anything for them when they had come home. They had gone through the ceremonies warriors had to go through to cleanse themselves of the horrors they'd seen and what they had had to do, and that was it. The Reservation was as poor as it had always been, and even the jobs the men had been able to find after the war were low paying jobs. She was totally against Elmer Guy, her son, going into the Marines.

Finding a Career Path

After giving up on his intention to become a Marine, Elmer started looking for a job. The problem he faced was a problem most Navajo have faced since the treaty period in Navajo history. Few jobs were available, and the competition for every one that did become available was fierce, and, though he did have one year of college under his belt, he didn't have a degree that gave him the entry credentials to become a professional.

After a somewhat desperate search, he finally got a job as a teacher's aide at the Chinle Valley School for Exceptional Children. Located in Chinle, the residential school served developmentally disabled students from throughout the Navajo Reservation. Students had a wide range of developmental disabilities ranging from deafness, developmental delays, emotional disturbances, intellectual disabilities, and what is now known as autism spectrum disorders.

What surprised the young teacher's aide is that he found the work both challenging and rewarding. The situations he found himself in could be stressful sometimes, especially when a student was "acting out," but more often, he felt like he was really making a difference in the lives of the students and professional staff. He did not feel out of place like he had at Northern Arizona. He was at home in Chinle with the people he understood and respected, and he was serving his tribe in a good way.

He had not been at the school for too long when he started developing projects that went beyond his basic duties. He heard about the Special Olympics program starting up in other parts of the country and got together with other staff members to get students at the school involved in Special Olympics. He worked one on one with several students and helped them progress toward more independent lives.

Finally, one of his favorite teachers at the school took him aside and told him that he was good at working with students. Then the teacher encouraged him to think about becoming a Special Education teacher. There was a shortage of such teachers throughout the country and especially in Indian country, he was told. If he chose to go to college and get his degree and certification, the teacher was pretty sure he had a solid future in front of him.

After that talk, Elmer started thinking about what he had been told and started looking into colleges that might have strong special education programs. He wasn't particularly anxious about leaving his job as a teacher's aide behind. He thought that he could probably return to the school after getting his degree as a teacher.

Finally, after searching through literature about several schools, he focused in on the University of Northern Colorado in Greeley, Colorado. Founded in 1889 between the Colorado Rockies and the Eastern Colorado plains, it had a strong reputation as having one of the finest special education teacher programs in the country. It's special education program seemed to be especially relevant to what Elmer wanted to enter so he could eventually serve the special education population in Navajo. He applied and, with letters of support from Chinle Valley School's teachers and administrators, was accepted.

After one semester at the university, however, he discovered the University of Arizona in Tucson had a matching grant program that would help him pay tuition, fees, and board. Northern Colorado was a good school, but it was expensive for a teacher's aide now a student from the Reservation. He wasn't sure how he was going to be able to afford earning a bachelor's degree there. He quickly filled out an application to transfer to Arizona and then filled out the paperwork to become a part of the matching grant program. When he was accepted both into the university and the program, he packed his bags and moved south to Tucson.

The University of Arizona

The first thing that impressed him about U of A was how big it was. Both Northern Arizona and Northern Colorado had been small schools in comparison even if he had thought both were huge. There were supposedly a lot of Navajo and other American Indian students on the Tucson campus, but the truth is that he hardly knew there were any Indians there. A center for Native students existed in the Old Main building, but it mostly existed for those who needed help with financial aid or had the time to belong to what seemed like a club set up to help students navigate their studies or the campus. His matching grant program gave him no problems, and he kept up his grades, so he determined early on that he'd concentrate on his studies.

The lectures in the classes were excellent, but the professors were demanding. Since his writing skills were still weak even after his experiences at Northern Arizona and Northern Colorado, he got in the habit of spending long hours in the library. One benefit was that the library was next to the football field, so, when he needed a break from trying to write a paper or master the content in a textbook or read an assigned book or article, he could watch the football game. He didn't feel confident enough in his studies to take the time to go to a game. In addition to the issue of cost (like a lot of other students from time immemorial, he didn't feel like he had any money), he didn't think he should spend that much time away from his efforts to get good grades.

He did long to go home and see his family and be back inside the comfort of people who understood what being Navajo meant, but the only time he could afford the long trip north since he didn't have access to a car to drive was primarily at Christmas. On his first Christmas home, his dad took him aside and told him that he was spending a lot of time trying to learn. Why was that taking him so long?

Elmer said that you had to think about education in terms of two. It took two years to get the idea about how to succeed at college in your head. Then you needed another two years to get your baccalaureate degree. After that you had to get a teaching job, spending two more years in the classroom. Then you could, if you'd worked really hard, become a principal and spend two years doing that. Then, after that, you could reach your goal of becoming a school superintendent.

In response, his dad just shook his head. He said that all the Navajo Elmer had gone to high school with had graduated and got jobs and got married and even had families. They had gotten on with life. What Elmer had done was spend his time away from home learning how to learn. His dad told him he'd better get busy, or he'd never catch up with the people that had been his friends.

Hearing what his dad had said, Elmer thought to himself that he had better really focus on what he was trying to achieve. He thought he could make a difference for the Navajo students who needed special services so they could live a better life, but he had to succeed at school first. Later, during another of his rare visits home, he told his younger siblings that they really needed to concentrate on school. That was where their futures were, but they would have to succeed in their studies if they were going to become what they could become.

As he wrapped up his studies at the university, the Special Education department assigned him to the Los Lunas Hospital and Training School in Los Lunas, NM to do his student teaching. The state school was dedicated to working with blind and deaf students. He discovered that working with non-Navajo students that had challenges in their lives was as satisfying as working with Navajo students back home. He felt like he was truly helping young people in their attempts to find a life for themselves.

Two and a half years after entering the University of Arizona, he graduated with his baccalaureate degree and certification in Special Education. He started applying for teaching positions not long before walking the stage in front of thousands of his fellow students and receiving his degree. He also applied for graduate school at the University of San Francisco that had the reputation of having one of the most advanced Rehabilitation Administration programs in the United States.

Almost immediately, Chinle Valley School for Exceptional Children offered him a teaching position. He was also accepted into the master's degree program in San Francisco where he would be expected to take residency for ten days on campus and work the rest of the time at Chinle Valley. The program was designed to have its students take what they were learning in the classroom to their jobs back home and do projects there that implemented concepts and ideas taken from their classes.

The Start of His Professional Career

Working at Chinle Valley as a fully certified Special Ed teacher was as satisfying as Elmer had imagined it would be when he had first applied to Northern Colorado. He was enormously busy as he pursued his graduate studies along with his daily teaching responsibilities. As he worked with the students and got immersed in the school's activities, however, feeling like he was making a difference for his people the way he had always dreamed of doing, two significant changes in his life were in the offing. One was not a surprise. The other set him on a different, unexpected course.

The first change was related to a young woman he had gotten to know at the university. Her brother and sister were at U of A along with Elmer. He had met them even though they were in different majors than he was. They had a sister, Martha, that Elmer had met. They were both studying Special Education, but she had not been in any classes with him. At the university, they had spent some time together. Martha had even borrowed a book after he'd taken a class she was just starting, so she wouldn't have to spend the money to buy it herself, but they parted ways when Elmer graduated with his degree and applied to Chinle Valley.

A year later Martha graduated. One of the first places she sent a job application was to Window Rock School District. She and Elmer then started their college relationship up again. When Martha received a job offer from the Window Rock District, their relationship deepened since they could easily see each other after a short drive between Chinle and Window Rock.

After they were engaged, however, something else happened. The Navajo Tribe in Window Rock had established a project for spinal cord injuries designed to help those who had been seriously injured to come back to Navajo after getting out of the hospital and then start what was called vocational rehabilitation. It was a sub-grant to a larger grant the newly created Navajo Vocational Rehabilitation Program (NVRP) had managed to put together with the State of Arizona. The idea was to work with individuals and help them learn how to manage their disability so they could live independently at home and even earn a living by developing marketable job skills.

The Director of the NVRP, after getting the subgrant, had learned that there was a young Navajo man enrolled in the rehabilitation program at University of San Francisco. He needed a director for the new project. When the Director contacted Elmer, Elmer wasn't sure he wanted to change the direction of his career. He was extraordinarily busy, and he liked what he was doing.

After thinking about the opportunity, though, he decided it might be too good to pass up. The salary was better, and he would be learning how grant projects worked. He'd also be in an administrative position, following through on the conversation about becoming a school superintendent he had had with his father years earlier. He resigned from Chinle Valley with some reluctance and took a leap of faith by taking the position he had been offered.

During this period, he proposed to Martha, and two years after he had graduated, they were married in Martha's hometown of Crystal, NM in a traditional ceremony where both families gathered and celebrated what would turn out to be a long and successful partnership. When Elmer is asked about what he first saw in Martha, he says that she was level-headed, intelligent, wise about their shared culture, would make a good mother, and could keep him on a good path to a good future.

Becoming the Director of Navajo Vocational Rehabilitation Program

Work at his new job was difficult. Before taking the job, he had insisted that he continue his graduate program and his studies while, at the same time, working at mastering the job. Working with the clients in the program was about all he could handle. He thought the job was vitally important for Navajo and was badly needed, but that did not mean it was not difficult.

Those he was working with had been sent home from the Denver Colorado Rehabilitation Center after they had been injured in car accidents or at rodeos. The project's concept was a good one but adjusting to such traumatic injuries often takes years. Accepting a severe disability once you've been a relatively healthy individual is extraordinarily difficult. Too often marriages fall apart, and drinking comes to seem like a good option for dealing with the emotional pain. The Bureau of Indian Affairs (BIA) provided housing for those returning from Denver, but the work for those trying to help the newly disabled clients was endless and often seemed desperate given the depth of the problems clients faced. Helping people fight their despair was an uphill battle.

Then Elmer became aware of a big problem not long after he had been hired. The main grant funding the NVRP only had a three-year window. The Spinal Injury Cord Project he had been hired under was a subgrant with the NVRP. The NVRP's primary grant had been negotiated with the State of Arizona Rehabilitation program when the state had decided continuing the state's operation of the rehabilitation effort on Navajo was not a good use of state resources. Navajo had lobbied for the project, and the state had decided it made sense to see if the Navajo Reservation could achieve the results expected. The problem was that the funds came through the state from the federal government, and no one had any idea if they would be renewed at the end of the grant term.

The good news was that the San Francisco graduate program was as good as its reputation said it was. In his classes, Elmer was learning about how the legislative process worked and was making contacts that would help him in his job, especially when it came to refunding the project.

Then, during the NVRP's second year of operation, the project Director left his position, and Elmer became the Deputy Director of Rehabilitation. A year later, as the arrangement with Arizona was nearing its end, the Assistant Director left. Elmer was given the job as Director. There was not much time left before the grant money dried up, but he had become an administrator and seemed to be achieving the ambition he had laid out to his father so many years before.

As soon as he got his new position, he started putting what he had learned in his graduate program to good use. He started working with members of the Arizona and New Mexico Congressional delegation, especially

Pete Domenici, one of the two senators from New Mexico.

Then he got to know William Natcher. Natcher was a powerful Congressman from Kentucky who chaired the House Subcommittee that oversaw rehabilitation programs. He was also known for his work on the House Appropriations Committee, where he played a crucial role in budgetary decisions about federal spending and was particularly noted for his expertise in matters related to health, education, and welfare, making significant contributions to legislation in these areas.

Congressman Natcher and Senator Domenici then got together and secured set-aside funding for Navajo Rehabilitation, saving Elmer's job as Director and continuing the tribe's role in developing rehabilitation programs, enlisting other Congresspeople in their effort. A set-aside is only short-term funding specially appropriated by Congress, so the long-term problem with funding still existed, but at least, for that time-period, Navajo was able to continue serving disabled people from Elmer's department.

After securing this first set-aside, Elmer kept working the halls of Congress as well as the tribal legislature. After the funding had been secured, Natcher had talked to Elmer and told him that, since he was the Chairman, he could not talk to the others on his committee about permanent funding for Navajo Rehabilitation, but he pointed out that Elmer could.

In the meantime, Elmer had gotten to know Ed Roberts, the head of the California Department of Rehabilitation. Roberts had been the victim of polio as a young child and was severely handicapped. He had also become a powerful advocate for disability rights, employment services for disabled people, community-based programs, and collaborations that could lead to better policies for disabled people around the country.

Roberts, through conversations with Elmer, found out about the need to get to members of Natcher's committee and introduced him to Ed Roybal, his Congressman in California. Roybal, the first Hispanic Congressman from Los Angeles, eventually introduce legislation Natcher could move forward to the full Congress as the set-asides Elmer kept pushing for became increasingly difficult to secure.

As all this was happening, Roberts worked with Elmer to integrate Navajo into the larger state and U.S. territory organizations administering rehabilitation programs and advocating for them throughout the country. During this time Navajo became, especially in relationships with the directors in California, Nevada, Hawaii, Arizona, Guam, and the Virgin Islands, an equal to powerful state rehabilitation programs.

The efforts coming out of Elmer's work in DC, at home in Navajo, and with Roberts and other rehabilitation leaders, especially in the west, led to a string of accomplishments that transformed rehabilitation services on Navajo. A timeline of this era, including an outline of the origin of the Navajo Rehabilitation program through the 1978 Rehabilitation Act reauthorization:

1975-1977: Arizona Division of Rehabilitation awarded a 3-year grant to the Navajo Nation to serve people with disabilities living on the reservation.

1978: A tri-state grant was entered into by State Vocational Rehabilitation Agencies from Arizona, New Mexico, and Utah to continue services.

An Intergovernmental Personnel Act (IPA) agreement was reached with the U.S. Rehabilitation Services Administration (RSA) that solidified Navajo Vocational Rehabilitation funding.

The Navajo Rehabilitation Department started applying for and getting other grants: for School to Work, Recreation, and Spinal Cord services.

The 1978 Rehabilitation Act was reauthorized that created Title 1, Part D, Section 130, authorizing the RSA Commission to award grants to Indian tribes.[7] Unfortunately, the RSA Commissioner never funded Section 130 even though up to one percent of the authorization was allowed for American Indian tribes.

Achieving Long-term
Vocational Rehabilitation Benefits for Navajo

During his tenure with the Navajo Nation Vocational Rehabilitation program from 1979-1992, Elmer helped secure vocational rehabilitation services for the Navajo people that have lasted to this day. Many of the grants achieved during that period required tribal matching funds, and the tribal legislature came through with those funds every time they were crucially needed. Total funding for NVRP increased from $650,000 to millions of dollars that funded over eighty vocational Rehabilitation programs.

Elmer also became involved in setting up major trust funds for handicapped members of the Nation, vocational education, and the elderly during this period. The tribe at that time had wanted to tax companies doing business inside the Navajo Reservation. The BIA, however, did not allow that, claiming that since the reservation was in Arizona and that the state taxed mineral leases, if the Navajo Reservation was allowed to levy its own taxes, the companies with the leases would be subject to dual taxation. Finally, Navajo sued the BIA and won a significant settlement when the United States Supreme Court in Kerr-McGee Corp. v. Navajo Tribe (471 U.S. 195 (1985) affirmed the Ninth Circuit's decision that no federal statute or principle of law mandated Department of Interior Secretarial approval when the Tribe decided to tax mineral lessees operating on the reservation.

One day Navajo Nation Chairman Peterson Zah took Elmer on a plane ride to Albuquerque and asked him what he would do if he suddenly had 20 million dollars to spend for disabled Navajos. Elmer responded that he would set up two trust funds, one of 10 million for handicapped services and another of an equal amount for vocational education. Mr. Zah listened to what Elmer had to say, but Elmer wasn't sure that anything would happen out of the conversation.

Then Mr. Zah came to his office in Window Rock one day and asked him to get as many handicapped people to the Council meeting the following day as possible. He was going to try to get the Council to go along with using funds from the court to set up three trust funds: 7 million dollars each for the handicapped, vocational education, and the elderly who really needed support too.

Elmer went to work and helped to pack the Council chambers with people with a variety of handicaps, and, after some complex political maneuvering and back and forth, 7 million dollars was set aside for the handicapped, 7 million for the elderly, and 6 million for vocational education, helping to improve services for each one of those groups over the long term.

An Important Accomplishment

One of Elmer's most important accomplishments occurred when he worked with Natcher to amend the Rehabilitation Act. Congressman Roybal made the initial request to add not less than one quarter of one percent and up to one percent of the act's appropriations for American Indian vocational programs. With Natcher pushing the amendment, it passed, and Congress approved the funding. This appropriation led to a Request for Proposals (RFP), and three Native projects were funded, including the one submitted by NVRP.

This year (2025), the American Indian Vocational Rehabilitation program will be celebrating its 50th anniversary. There are ninety-three American Indian Vocational Rehabilitation Services projects funded by the Rehabilitation Act, Title 1 across 26 states that receive roughly four million dollars in appropriations.

Executive Director, Division of Diné Education

As he worked to build Vocational Rehabilitation, tribal politics began to play an increasingly important role in Elmer's life. No one in administration can avoid politics. When funding and the use of resources becomes involved, political maneuvering becomes as inevitable as sunrise.

The intensity of politics really began affecting his life when Peter McDonald was removed as the Chairman of the Navajo Nation by the tribal council in 1989. Chairman McDonald supported Elmer as he built the rehabilitation program, but then the Bureau of Indian Affairs, after McDonald had served four terms as Chairman,[8] started criminal investigations against the former Code Talker. These investigations led to the Council's termination decision, which led to the appointment of an Interim Chairman, Leonard Haskie. This led to a shakeup of the tribe's organization as all the Division Directors were removed from their posts, including the Director of Navajo Education. Dr. Rena Yazzie, a prominent Navajo educator, was appointed as the Acting Director, and she asked Elmer to help her manage the Division.

Elections for a new Chairman were then held, and Peterson Zah won. After Chairman Zah was inaugurated, he assigned Elmer as Acting Director of the Navajo Division of Education while he evaluated the administration of all the divisions and departments of the Nation. In the end, he did not hire Elmer as the director, but by that time Elmer had become an expert on the Division and had started developing ideas about how to improve Navajo education whether it was being delivered by public schools, BIA schools, private schools, or tribal schools.

He also secured a four-million-dollar grant from the Ford Foundation for a Teacher's Training initiative. Nearly all the teachers working with Navajo students were non-Navajo and, in too many cases, even those teachers did not have majors in math and science subjects where test scores by students were especially weak. The effort supported by the Ford grant was to begin the process of creating a growing number of Navajo teachers while strengthening the performance by the teaching staff then in place in schools working with Navajo students.

Then, Peterson Zah, whom Elmer had become loyal to and worked to re-elect, lost his re-election bid. He had done so many things to strengthen the Navajo

Nation that he would be honored for the rest of his life even though some of his actions did not sit well with a majority of the Navajo people voting in that election. Albert Hale became the President. He appointed a new Executive Director for Navajo Education, Anita Tsinnijinnie. Then she asked Elmer to help her as the Deputy Director.

Elmer, feeling conflicted, called Peterson Zah, who, typically, told him Albert Hale was a good man and urged him to accept the appointment. Elmer accepted the position. Not long after that, Chairman Hale let Director Tsinnijinnie go after leading educators started objecting to some of her policies and actions and appointed Elmer the Executive Director of Diné Education.

Navajo Education

Elmer would serve as the Executive Director for just under a year. Navajo political winds kept lifting Chairmen up and then sending them down the road. Those who served in politically appointed positions were then removed so the new Chairman could appoint his own people.

The job of the Executive Director, or even Deputy Director, of Navajo Education was a huge one. The Diné lived in one of the least educated parts of the United States. On any measure of educational attainment, number of college or high school graduates, dropout or daily school attendance rates, or employment rates after school completion, the Navajo people lagged far behind any segment of the population in Arizona, New Mexico, or Utah.

The complexity of the Navajo educational ecosystem presented another challenge since the leadership of Navajo education had to work with tribal, state, BIA, religious school, and private school administrators and Boards of Education if they hoped to improve educational attainment of Navajo students. This did not even address significant numbers of unemployed people on the Reservation that needed to gain job skills training necessary to find a job.

As his responsibilities grew, Elmer found that his time working with his grandparents as a shepherd had taught him a lot of useful life lessons. You not only had to be watchful and aware of what was happening in the environment around the sheep as a herder, but you also had to be patient and willing to be insistent if you wanted the sheep to do what you wanted them to do.

Working in tribal, regional, or national politics required similar attributes. Nothing was going to happen overnight just because you had determined that it was the right thing to do to move things forward. You also had to be patient, extremely aware of the political currents surrounding and inside whatever legislature with which you were working. If you pushed too hard at the wrong moment, all your efforts would scatter, and then you would have to make an enormous effort to move forward with what you wanted to achieve all over again.

When he became the Executive Director, he had achieved what he had told his father he'd intended to achieve back when he had been at the University of Arizona. He was not exactly a Superintendent, but he was working in concert with superintendents from schools in the Nation and border towns, as well as principals, chairs of school boards, and departmental leaders in agencies and department that could affect what happened to Navajo students. As the Executive Director, he administered over 43 million dollars in federal, state, tribal, and private and foundation grants, adhered to pertinent policies and procedures he inherited that had been developed over decades of legislative and department decisions, presented testimony at Congressional and state hearings, and sought additional resources.

Significant Accomplishments as Executive Director

His biggest accomplishment during his term came when he was instrumental in securing a ten-million-dollar grant from the National Science Foundation (NSF) to strengthen science, math, and technology education. Thomas Atcitty, Hale's Vice President, a former President of Navajo Community College, was especially helpful in Elmer's efforts to improve science, math, and technology education during his tenure as Executive Director, including in the writing and securing of the NSF grant. If Navajo student reading scores were below national averages, math scores were even more problematic. Too often math, science, and technology teachers in schools serving Navajo students did not even have the qualifications expected in those fields. The NSF grant was designed to supplement the education students were receiving in schools with experiential activities, tutoring, and other projects designed to improve their mastery of subjects supported by the grant.

Elmer also helped secure a one-million-dollar grant from the Annenberg Foundation to strengthen school and community partnerships. Looking out at the ecosystem of Navajo education, Elmer thought that part of the problem with student performance came out of the distrust of schools originating in the boarding school movement. The treaties signed by the Navajo and other tribes guaranteed education would be a central service received in return for the American seizure of land and resources effected during the Indian wars. The boarding schools were part of how the U.S. government had implemented this treaty promise, taking young children from their homes and then demanding they lose their culture and language and even given names as they ended up in a large building where they did as much time doing labor as they spent in the classroom or studying. The extent of disorientation and suffering caused by the boarding schools is still coming to light as graveyards with unmarked graves of children are uncovered and records of child abuse are brought out into the light of day.

With the Annenberg grant, Elmer was hoping to involve Navajo communities more fully into the schools that served them, taking a step toward making school attendance and performance more acceptable throughout Navajo. If the Navajo people and families took responsibility for Navajo education, he reasoned, then the students from the communities that felt more involved would take their schoolwork more seriously and perform better.

Unfortunately, before Elmer hardly had the chance to put his efforts in motion, his tenure as Executive Director ended when Albert Hale resigned his presidential position and elected not to run in the next election. Elmer had climbed to the top rung of the ladder of Navajo education responsibility, but he was dependent upon the political winds to keep the position he'd achieved.

At Navajo Community College

As the Executive Director of Navajo Education, one of Elmer's duties was to serve on the Board of Regents of Navajo Community College (NCC), the first tribal college in the country and one of the most prestigious. Elmer knew there was little chance he would be able to retain his position as the Executive Director once Chairman Hale resigned. Tommy Lewis, the President of NCC, talked to him during the interim period after the election and before the new President had finalized putting his cabinet together and asked if Elmer might consider coming to work at the college.

Dr. Lewis was one of the most impressive tribal college leaders in the country, a powerful voice in the American Indian Higher Education Consortium (AIHEC) and a participant in nearly all the efforts to strengthen the TCU movement during one of the movement's most important historical periods. He thought Elmer could help him by becoming part of the fund-raising team he was trying to strengthen to help secure the college's long-term future. He was impressed by both the NSF and foundation grants Elmer had achieved during his term as Deputy and Executive Director at the tribe.

After Elmer received the formal notice that his successor had been appointed, he accepted Dr. Lewis's job offer. NCC headquarters is in Tsaile, Arizona, the same place where the Guys had a ranch where Elmer raised a few cattle and where he often spent his free time feeding livestock and keeping the place in good repair. He had loved the area as a child, and now he would be working close to where the ranch was located.

The first task he was given by Dr. Lewis was to work with the tribal legislature to see if tribal funds could be invested on an annual basis into NCC and CIT, the second tribal college on the reservation. Navajo was the only tribe in the United States with two TCUs. NCC had been the first tribal college, and CIT had been formed as part of the first cohort of TCUs. They had both become members of AIHEC before the Tribally Controlled Community Colleges Assistance Act of 1978 had been passed. Neither were funded primarily through the allocations provided through that act. Therefore, Navajo was not limited to one TCU the way other tribes were through that legislation.[9]

By this time, Elmer knew most of the Navajo legislators and had significant experience at getting legislation passed through both the tribal legislature and even the Congress of the United States. Starting in at NCC, he wasted no time in getting an effort started to provide the first tribal funding that either NCC or CIT had ever received. Because of what had been achieved during the Peter McDonald and Peterson Zah administrations, the Navajo Nation did have considerable resources. Peterson Zah had even set up an investment fund that was quickly growing its principle into sums never seen before in Indian country.

Still, Elmer had no illusions. Getting the tribal council and the President to pass the necessary legislation, obligate the funding, and then sign the legislation was not going to be an easy task. Improving Navajo higher education institutions might be an important goal, but every chapterhouse inside the Navajo Nation had needs for housing, electricity, water, buildings, roads, infrastructure, law enforcement, and on and on. The Head Start programs were struggling, and the K-12 systems all had needs. In the end, Navajo resources, although they had been built up over the years, were still a fraction of what was needed to really improve the future for all the Diné people.

Then, as Elmer started working on what was going to be a difficult task and began to get involved in other funding raising efforts at NCC, he learned of an intriguing position opening at CIT. As the Executive Director of Education, he had been involved in the accreditation review at CIT. CIT did not hold institution of higher education accreditation from the North Central Agency that the federal government recognized as the official accreditor for New Mexico colleges and universities. Rather, it held accreditation as a special function school, which was more associated with high schools than colleges. During his review of CIT accreditation, he had questioned why it had not pursued full college accreditation. As he thought about the opening at the school, he also thought about the promise inherent in what CIT could become.

Jim Tutt, President of CIT

Jim Tutt had been the President for nearly all of CIT's existence. Like Dr. Lewis, he was highly respected in AIHEC and was effective in his work with the federal agencies that funded CIT. He had moved the organization from being a job training center for the tribe to a college that offered vocational and technical certificates recognized by the North Central Association's accreditation authority. The college had just started the process of offering associate of applied science degrees, the next step in becoming a full-fledged accredited institution of higher learning.

Both Mr. Tutt and Dr. Lewis had also been important voices in achieving land grant status for the tribal colleges that existed in 1994. The nation's land grant system had been created by the Morrill Acts of 1862 and 1890.[10] Basically, the United States government assigned land to the states to create the universities founded because of the 1862 act. Most of the land used to create the 1862s had at one point been American Indian land seized because of westward expansion and the Indian wars. The land grant universities quickly became powerful in each of the states. By the time the tribal colleges began seeking land grant status, the state university land grants were not only the most prestigious teaching and learning institution of higher learning in each state but also a center of academic research, especially in agriculture and the trades.

Securing land grant status for the tribal colleges was not easy. Most of what are known as the 1862 land grant universities opposed bringing tribal colleges into the system. They were afraid there were so many small tribal colleges that they would compete with them for funding. The 1890 historically black colleges and universities that were land grant institutions were much more open to the tribal colleges, but the effort led by AIHEC and leaders like Mr. Tutt and Dr. Lewis, and especially Dr. Joe McDonald of Salish Kootenai College, took years of effort with both the 1862s and Congress.

The Dean of Instruction Position

The job open at CIT was for a Dean of Instruction. This was clearly a step up from what Elmer was doing for Dr. Lewis. He had been learning a lot about higher education both during his stints as Deputy and Executive Director for the Navajo Nation and his time at NCC. After thinking about the possibility of becoming a Dean of Instruction, he submitted his application.

Once the application was in, however, Elmer was not a shoo-in for the position. Mr. Tutt had his reservations about bringing in a former Executive Director of Education for the tribe into a dean position. Elmer's academic background was in vocational rehabilitation, not education, and certainly not in higher education academic affairs. Mr. Tutt was also under pressure at the Department of Education and BIA to get CIT accredited as a community college. The accreditation the college held was more in line with a high school's accreditation, and by this time most of the tribal colleges, after a long struggle,[11] had achieved full higher education accreditation. Elmer had served on the Navajo Nation State Board for North Central Accreditation of Schools, but higher education accreditation was much more rigorous and difficult to attain. CIT had already tried to become accredited and not succeeded. The new Dean was going to have to succeed.

CIT's Board of Directors did not have any misgivings about Elmer's application, however. His success at building funding through the Congress, federal agencies, and private foundations was impressive to say the least. The Tribal Council was also well-disposed toward him, which could help the college as it went forward, trying to fulfill the promise Mr. Tutt had managed to make possible. He might not have the traditional credentials of a Dean of Instruction, but he certainly had the skills and attributes that could be helpful to Mr. Tutt and the institution as it evolved into an increasingly important college.

In the end, Mr. Tutt called Elmer into his office in Crownpoint one day and offered him the job. Excited about this new opportunity, Elmer accepted.

At CIT

Once he had started his new position, Elmer proved what he had gotten used to proving. Despite Mr. Tutt's misgivings, the two of them got along collegially, starting a partnership that looked like it might be successful. Elmer was always quiet and even tempered. Mr. Tutt was much more animated and forceful in his animation. Elmer was skilled at listening and thinking about what Mr. Tutt was saying and then coming up with a course of actions that helped lead them to accomplishing what had to be done.

Mr. Tutt had led the way to a long list of accomplishments for the college. The Crownpoint campus was extensive with a cafeteria that attracted community people as well as providing a place for students to gather. He had also managed to construct two large dorm buildings that had turned the workforce development institution into a residential college. The number of different credentialled programs and associate degrees had also steadily increased under his leadership. By the time Elmer started his new position, certificates or associate degrees had been launched for areas like Culinary Arts, Law Advocate, Early Childhood Education, and Certified Nursing Assistant, ranging far afield from the institution's early focus on construction trades and secretarial skills.

One of Mr. Tutt's most impressive accomplishments was the Veterinary Hospital, a little removed from the main campus, that provided services to the community in and around Crownpoint and offered a Veterinary Technician Certificate program. He had managed to hire one of the most important veterinarians from Gallup, NM, Clint Balok, to run the hospital and education program who, after he was hired, became an important voice in the national TCU land grant community. He had also built up enough sources of funding to put the college on a solid financial foundation.

There were some serious challenges. The accreditation problem loomed large as Elmer first started organizing his office in one of the mobile classroom units that littered the campus. One of the problems was that too many of the instructors did not have a master's degree or the full qualifications necessary for their role as professional instructors. The fledgling college also did not have the reputation possessed by NCC in the community. NCC was considered a real college even though not everyone among Navajo educated population believed tribal education centered in Navajo culture and language was the way to help Navajo improve its economic standing in competition with the non-Indian communities in Arizona, New Mexico, and Utah.

CIT was often dismissed as an "Indian college," a second-rate school pretending to be something it was not. There was a lot of talk about drug and alcohol problems on campus. These were not as bad as the rumors going around suggested they were, but the rumors did not help the college's reputation. The staff was also "stove-piped," grouped into cliques that often sat together during lunch, ignoring other groups of faculty members sitting around them. Too many had their own agendas that did not always agree with Mr. Tutt's vision of where he wanted to take the institution.

What had been achieved at CIT by that point in time was impressive despite its challenges. Still, as Elmer got increasingly familiar with what was going on, he knew that both he and Mr. Tutt had their work cut out for them. If he was going to be involved in the college, he wanted to build both its capabilities and reputation, creating one of the best higher education institutions among the nation's TCUs. He knew this might take a while, but he was also convinced he had the ability to play a strong role in making that happen. After all, look at what he'd accomplished when he became a grant director for the tribe's Vocational Rehabilitation grant program. It now was firmly established alongside state rehabilitation programs as a showcase among the rehab programs offered by over 80 tribes throughout the United States.

The Kellogg Foundation Grant

One part of CIT that Elmer was not that aware of at first was the stirring controversy about Clint Balok and a grant he and Mr. Tutt had secured from the Kellogg Foundation. During 1994, the foundation had developed the largest philanthropic grant program that had ever been designed for TCUs. Called The Kellogg Native American Higher Education Initiative, grants awarded to individual colleges were to strengthen institutions and mobilize change in such a way as to help the colleges help themselves, as Betty Overton, the Director of Higher Education at Kellogg put it.[12]

Dr. Balok was enamored of the idea of raising elk as a herd animal the way the Navajo raised sheep and cattle, and he convinced Mr. Tutt that he could write a successful Kellogg Foundation proposal around elk that would achieve the highest foundation funding possible. Attracting Dr. Balok to CIT had been a major coup, improving CIT's standing in both the Crownpoint area and nationally, especially within the land grant system and the Department of Agriculture. After consideration, Mr. Tutt gave the approval to go ahead with the proposal. Dr. Balok knew several western tribes were creating buffalo herds in much the same way he wanted to create an elk herd, and he positioned the proposal as an economic development effort for the Navajo. When Kellogg reviewed the proposal, CIT became one of the big winners in the initiative.

The problem was that elk are considered a sacred animal among the Navajo. Navajo men must go through ceremonies to hunt them and then offer specific prayers after a successful hunt. As Dr. Balock developed the project and word of what was happening started to filter out into the Navajo Nation, traditional voices in the tribe began to object. Medicine men were especially strong in their objection. As Elmer became familiar with the project in his new role, he shared what he was hearing with Mr. Tutt, but Mr. Tutt, feeling loyal to Dr. Balock, ignored what Elmer was telling him. He felt the elk project was a good one. Since Elmer was new in his position, he put his disquiet aside so that he could support CIT's President.

Mastering the Job of a Dean of Instruction
and then Academic Vice President

As he settled into his new job, Elmer concentrated on getting to know the faculty he was now responsible to oversee. At the tribe he had managed small groups of employees, but CIT's faculty was the largest number of people he had administrative responsibility for up to that time. He also continued his efforts, started at NCC, to get tribal funding for both CIT and NCC even if Mr. Tutt was skeptical that the effort could succeed. He thought there were just too many needs on the Reservation for the two colleges to take precedence for funding, especially given the federal monies the colleges were able to access.

Three other projects also took up his time. There was the critical effort to achieve the first step in NCA[13] accreditation, Candidacy for Accreditation, and two important federal sources of funding were hanging fire. The National Science Foundation (NSF) had told CIT that a 2 million dollar plus proposal submitted under its Tribal College and University's Program (TCUP) could be funded if it was improved, and a similar message had been delivered from the Department of Education based upon a Title III, Strengthening Institutions grant Mr. Tutt had used his political acumen in DC to push for funding.

Achieving Candidacy for Accreditation, Elmer quickly learned, was significantly more demanding than the accreditation he had helped achieve by working with K-12 school systems in the Navajo Department of Education. Success depended upon doing a self-study that would examine all aspects of the college's operations against five major criteria required of all colleges and universities in the North Central Region of the United States. The self-study process required the faculty, administration, financial office, and every other aspect of the college to be involved in developing the required document. One other effort had been made to achieve Candidacy status that had not succeeded. This time CIT needed to succeed.

The two grant programs meant millions of dollars in funding for CIT and could help move the college to a new level of capability and success. Elmer had succeeded in working with NSF at the tribal level, so he knew Jody Chase, the program officer who often championed American Indian proposals, especially for the TCUs. He had also worked with the Department of Education, although Mr. Tutt's contacts were stronger than his when it came to TCU funding.

To handle the volume of work, he moved into a small apartment on campus and started traveling home to be with his family in Window Rock on weekends. He also started to realize that his new job was going to require a lot of travel to participate in AIHEC events and move projects forward both with the federal government and the tribe. He was determined to succeed, however, and he undertook to meet all the demands on him with his usual calm demeanor and willingness to work hard.

Accreditation and NSF TCUP

To tackle the self-study, Mr. Tutt appointed a Self-Study Committee and put Elmer in charge. Then they assigned a staff member who was Navajo to write the required report. As that work started, Elmer called Jody Chase in DC and asked her what needed to be done to get the NSF proposal on track. She told him that CIT needed to put the goals and objectives in the grant into a five-year master plan. Then, after talking to Elmer about what NSF expected, she recommended he hire a consultant, which, after several days of research he did. He hired Tom Davis, who had helped found the College of the Menominee Nation and worked with Carrie Billy, the Navajo Executive Director on the White House Initiative on Tribal College and Universities for President Bill Clinton, to get the NSF TCUP program in place. Davis agreed to come to Crownpoint for thirty days to redo the original proposal and get it accepted by NSF.

Once on campus, Davis gathered all the science, technology, and math faculty together, and, with Elmer directing what was happening, developed a proposal that refashioned what was then known as science, math, education, and technology (SMET)[14] education at CIT and positioned those programs to add strength to its academic offerings, creating a college that had both strong trades programs as well as academic programs. When NSF approved the newly refashioned proposal, CIT then had the funding to begin its ascendancy, over time, to the status of being one of the most prestigious minority serving institutions of higher education in the United States.

After the project was approved, Elmer then proceeded to talk Davis into staying on board to manage the project for six months, calling him into his office to talk him into staying for thirty more days when he kept indicating he was going to go back home to Carlton, Minnesota where he had lived until he had left his job at Fond du Lac Tribal and Community College. This continued until Davis was offered the Presidency at Little Priest Tribal College in Nebraska.

In the meantime, the work on Candidacy continued. A self-study report was developed, and Elmer, afraid that it wasn't strong enough, asked Mr. Tutt to bring in a mock-Accreditation-Review Board to see if they were ready to go forward. The clock was ticking since CIT had informed NCA what they were doing and had a timeframe in which they had to submit the self-study. After Elmer assembled a team of outside accreditation experts, the review team came on campus. Their report was disastrous. CIT should cancel their current effort to become a Candidate, Elmer and Mr. Tutt were told. They were not even close to being ready.

Mr. Tutt was, to say the least, upset by the report of the mock team that had been hired. Elmer didn't fully realize how much pressure Mr. Tutt was receiving from DC to get the college accredited. The Carl Perkins program, which was the largest funding source for CIT's trades programs, was becoming increasingly insistent that the college become fully accredited. Elmer wasn't pleased about what their efforts had achieved either, but he didn't panic. He brought in Davis, who had delivered Candidacy to the College of Menominee Nation, to help replan and rewrite the report, working with him and the other staff that had been involved in the effort, and pushed to get ready to meet NCA's deadline. Through an enormous effort, the self-study report was re-researched and redone and submitted by the deadline.

The result of the Accreditation team's visit to the campus that happened a few months later was not perfect. The self-study report had reported many of the weaknesses in the college's operations, and the NCA team identified others. However, the team recommended that CIT be awarded Candidacy status, although their recommendation had language that hedged on their recommendation.

After the team's report was reviewed at the NCA's Chicago headquarters, Mr. Tutt and Elmer were invited to defend their Candidacy application before the Board that would have to approve it. This did not happen for stronger applicants, but there were a lot of questions about whether CIT deserved to be approved.

The trip to Chicago went as well as could have been hoped. The Board had several questions for both Mr. Tutt and Elmer. They were not given a decision after their appearance had been completed, but a few months after that, the approval letter arrived in Crownpoint, giving CIT Candidacy for Accreditation.

Achieving Tribal Funding for CIT and NCC at Last

While all of this was being accomplished, Elmer also delivered on the project Tommy Lewis had originally assigned him and that Mr. Tutt had not believed could happen. Elmer had first tried to get funding for the two colleges while still the Executive Director of Education for the tribe. He had made a presentation to the Education Committee about the desirability of supporting the two higher education institutions. They had agreed, and then Chairman Hale had given the go-ahead.

The idea was that the fuel excise tax would be increased, and the increase in funds generated would be used to fund the colleges and scholarships. The Navajo Tax Commission had to support the proposal, but Elmer managed to get that approval. After that the tax increase had to go before the Navajo people for a referendum vote. When that vote was successful, Elmer, Dr. Lewis, and Mr. Tutt all were excited.

Then Chairman Hale left the Chairmanship, and Elmer lost his position as the Executive Director. He took the job at NCC instead. As he took up his new position, the new Attorney General appointed by the new Tribal Chairman, Kelsey A. Begaye, reviewed the legislation and ruled that the fuel excise tax could not be used to fund education programs. The legislation could not be implemented.

By then Elmer was at NCC. Dr. Lewis appointed him to secure funding for the two colleges despite the setback. He got busy and started working on getting funding without using the fuel excise tax. The going was difficult. What had been put into place and killed was difficult to revive. Then he took the Dean position at CIT.

As he worked on his other priorities, he got together with the President at NCC that replaced Dr. Lewis when he was terminated, Dr. Ferlin Clark. The two of them worked together to draft new legislation, the Diné Higher Education Grant Fund Act, that they took to the Council. At first, they were going to push for five years of funding, but then Elmer decided that since Navajo law allowed for 20-year funding cycles, they should go for the maximum instead. Then, to Mr. Tutt's surprise, after spending what seemed countless hours talking to Council members and attending meetings in Window Rock, the legislation passed, giving CIT 4.2 million dollars a year and NCC 4.7 million.

The two colleges now have different names. CIT is NTU and NCC is Diné College, but 2025 is the year when the 20-year life of the grants end. Currently Diné College and Elmer are again working together, trying to maintain this source of funding so that it becomes permanent.

An Accredited College Embroiled in Controversy

The year that followed CIT achieving the first step toward full accreditation turned out to be complex. On one hand, Elmer got more comfortable in his role with the college. Academics at the college continued to develop in the way he had envisioned after achieving the NSF grant and Candidacy.

Mr. Tutt, however, faced increasing pressure from the Board of Directors. The Board was not happy about the elk project. When it became known that the elk were being placed on Dr. Balok's private land where Kellogg Foundation funds had been used to make some of the improvements necessary, the criticism increased. When the word went out that Dr. Balok had purchased some of his own elk and mixed them with CIT elk, objection to the project exploded.

Whatever Mr. Tutt, after well over a decade of service, recommended to the Board was automatically sharply questioned. The Title III grant had approved money for constructing a Culinary Arts Center, which was desperately needed. The program was operating out of a small, inadequate kitchen in the cafeteria building and didn't even have real classroom space. When the architectural and engineering work was submitted to the Board for approval, they opposed what had been done, and the project was delayed. On issue after issue, board members asked questions, showing they no longer had confidence in the President.

Elmer was settling into his job in higher education, but he did not want to be on the wrong side of Mr. Tutt even though, as a traditional Navajo man, he did not agree with the wisdom of the elk project. His calm demeanor served him well during this tumultuous time. He refused to take a stand against Mr. Tutt but also made sure he listened carefully to the Board and followed what they wanted him to do.

Finally, the entire matter came to a head. The Board was done with Mr. Tutt. In recognition of his long service to the college, they would accept him as the provost of the college, but they would no longer accept him in the top role. Then they asked Elmer to follow Mr. Tutt as the President. An arrangement like that was bound to be awkward, but Elmer accepted their appointment, and Mr. Tutt took the job offered to him. The arrangement was not destined to last for long, but it did calm things down for at least a while.

President Elmer Guy

At the beginning of his presidency, Dr. Guy was the head of a small TCU that had the status of a land grant institution of higher education but had only just achieved Candidacy status. It did not have a sterling reputation in the Navajo Nation as a whole, though it was a better institution than the credit it was often given. Less than 340 students were enrolled. The science labs were being improved through the NSF grant, but both the technology infrastructure at the college was substandard and the labs available for students still were not where they needed to be if the school was to strengthen its science education long-term.

High bandwidth Internet connectivity seemed like an impossible dream because of the rural nature of the campus. There were no fiber lines available to Crownpoint. The college did not even offer a course in calculus. Even some of the math teachers had the opinion that Navajo students had a strong aversion to math and could not be expected to become competent enough to pass higher math courses.

Too many of the faculty also did not have the qualifications even expected in technical colleges in the U.S. A few of the trades' instructors had some experience in their field but did not possess even an associate degree. Too few of the academic instructors had master's degrees in their field. All these challenges were pointed out as areas that needed to be improved through the NCA Candidacy for Accreditation process.

Elmer believed in the college's promise. Significant numbers of students were achieving their certificates, especially from the trades' programs, every year. An increasing number were earning associate degrees. General Education had been strengthened during the preparations for Candidacy, and the faculty, if undereducated for their positions, were still good instructors and believed in the school. Most of them understood that they needed to improve their credentials if they were to remain in their jobs, and most of them had already started the process of strengthening their qualifications.

The new NSF program was also strengthening science and math education, which had at one point been the softest parts of the curriculum. It had also launched a new technology curriculum that would lead to an associate of applied science in Information Technology.

One of Elmer's earliest moves occurred when he brought in a new Dean of Instruction who would have the responsibility for working with the faculty to introduce new curriculum and strengthen their credentials. The new Dean would also be responsible for achieving full accreditation and moving the college beyond its Candidacy status. He hired Tom Davis, the former consultant on the NSF TCUP project, who resigned from his position as the President of Little Priest Tribal College to take the job. From that point on, Dr. Guy began working to implement his vision of driving Crownpoint Institute of Technology toward becoming one of the finest minority serving institutions of higher learning in the United States.

During the next several years, the accomplishments came at a steady pace. Jim Tutt, after an honorable career at CIT, left to head up an organization dedicated to providing dental service throughout the Navajo Nation. Shortly after the new Dean was hired, CIT became a fully accredited college. Then a series of new federally and state funded projects were achieved. The Internet to the Hogan Project brought high bandwidth wireless technology to the campus. The technology infrastructure started to rival that of any other community college in New Mexico and then started to rival the infrastructures in place at major universities around the country. A new state-of-the art Culinary Arts Center was built. An aggressive "build-your-own" employee incentive program was launched to help both instructors and staff earn the credentials needed at a respectable college. Then an emphasis on hiring PhD instructors with research abilities was initiated. During this process Elmer completed his own doctoral work and received his Doctor of Rehabilitation degree from the University of Arizona in 2009.

As each accomplishment was put into place, the strength of the college strengthened. The community college became Navajo Technical College in 2006 after the first bachelor of applied science degrees were launched in Information Technology, Digital Manufacturing, and New Media. The new degree programs required Calculus for graduation. Then the college became a university. Tom Davis wrote a poem that described the moment Elmer announced to a huge audience, including several candidates for President of the Navajo Nation, the real scope of his vision for the future:

How to Not Fall Off a Stage During Commencement

Falling backwards off a high stage while sitting in a chair
is probably not the best way to live a life,
but we were in Chinle, Arizona
having our first graduation commencement where
Navajo Technical College,
formerly the Crownpoint Institute of Technology,
had established its first instructional site
away from the main campus in Crownpoint, New Mexico.

A huge crowd of Navajo rose in rows
out of the deep well of Chinle High School gymnasium,
including all the candidates for the Navajo presidency
and a host of other chapterhouse delegate politicians.
I had been placed on the stage close to a four-foot drop to
    the gym's floor.

As Elmer Guy, the President who had drawn me to the
    Navajo Nation,
got up to speak as commencement exercises and ceremony
swirled with the deep spirit of who the Diné are,
I was reflecting back on what Elmer, I,

and the rest of the college had accomplished.
When Elmer had first hired me,
the Crownpoint Institute of Technology
had a student body of three hundred and thirty-three
    students.
I had been stunned, when I first went to community events,
to discover how little people thought of the school.
It's just a pretend college, they had said,
a place where students can get away from home and go
    wild.

Now, we had succeeded in turning around Navajo Nation
    opinion enough
to attract the tribe's most prominent leaders to a
    commencement.

As Elmer walked, with the calm dignity he has always
    exuded,
     to the microphone,
I smiled to myself, thinking he really was somebody worth
    following.
He was as solid as red cliffs that rose into
Crownpoint's New Mexico skies.
He started to speak in his soft voice,
and I looked intently at the huge crowd.
This was really quite a day.

Then, suddenly, I heard, really heard, what he was saying.
"We are going to become the first Navajo University," he
    said.

A university? Really? We'd not talked about that.
We'd just barely become a college.
I'd just told Elmer the technology staff, faculty, and I
were beginning to work on a baccalaureate degree.

Forgetting about the drop off behind me,

I scooted the chair I was sitting on, a little in shock,
backwards.
Putting together a university had to be a huge challenge.
What the . . .
Dr. Larry Isaac, on one side of me,
and Delores Becenti on the other side,
shot out hands as unobtrusively as they could manage
as my chair started to tip backwards.
Stabilized, I scooted forward a bit and acted
like nothing had happened.
There are dreams, though,
and sometimes dreams come true
even when they almost tip you off a high stage.

Later, after we'd established a half dozen baccalaureate
    degrees
and been approved to offer a master's degree
in Diné Culture, Language, and Leadership,
Elmer told me that he'd, just on the spur of the moment,
    looking out at the crowd,
decided to wake everybody up.

At Navajo Technical University everybody is working
toward endless possibilities.[15]

By the time Navajo Technical College had become a
university, it had achieved a new NSF TCUP grant that
allowed the development and launch of its first
engineering programs in Industrial and Electrical
Engineering. Other programs were also offering
bachelor's degrees, and the first master's degree in Diné
Culture, Language, and Leadership was in the
development stage. Not long after that NTU became the
first TCU to offer a PhD research degree in Diné (Navajo)
Culture and Language Sustainability. By this time,
Elmer's dream of having a Navajo university that was a

full-fledged research university was a reality, and NTU was one of the most respected minority-serving institutions of higher learning in the United States.

Challenges arose periodically during the years it took to accomplish all of this. One of the most serious was when Bureau of Indian Affairs funding, which at that time constituted close to 40% of the college's budget, was threatened in DC., Elmer and his staff, in response, organized letter writing campaigns by students and faculty in support of the college, got chapterhouses throughout the Navajo nation involved, worked extensively with the Navajo Nation advocacy office in DC, and then joined forces with David Gipp, then the President of United Tribes Technical College and one of the most significant TCU leaders in the nation, and convinced Congress and the President to pass legislation that protected the funding the two colleges shared. The funding had originally been designed to further Reservation economic development through technical education. The new legislation strengthened that mission which had always been central to Elmer's vision for the college.

As each of the challenges rose, whether it was at the tribal, state, or national levels or inside the college itself, Elmer worked through the problem by getting his staff together, laying out the challenge, and then achieving whatever needed to be achieved. As the college grew into a university, he repeated this pattern again and again, increasing the college's budget, its programs, and its research strength in the process.

An International Reputation

Traveling the road toward success at Navajo Technical University, Dr. Guy has also carved out an international reputation as a leading U.S. educator. A list of some of the accomplishments he has recorded nationally and internationally is as follows:

2025-Present, Board Member of the Higher Learning Commission Board of Trustees.

2024-Present, Co-Chair for the National Congress of American Indian Education Subcommittee.

2012-2021 to Present Served as Chairperson of the Community College Advisory Panel for the College Board representing Minority Community Colleges. Co-chaired the 2018 College Board Forum. After 2018 he became a Trustee member of the college board for three years.

2006 to Present, Board Member of the American Indian Higher Education Consortium. Currently serves as the President for 37 Tribal Colleges and Universities after serving as the Vice Chairman of the Executive Committee. He was on the following Committees: US. Department of Agriculture Leadership, Finance, and Tribal College Journal of American Indian Higher Education and still serves on Finance and the college journal.

2011 to Present Board Member to the World Indigenous Nations Higher Education Consortium. He served two terms as the Co-Chair of the WINHEC Executive Committee, an international support organization for Indigenous Peoples from 7 countries, including United States that pursues goals common to indigenous controlled member institutions of higher learning through higher education.

2009 to 2018 Board Member to the American Indian College Fund. Completed 9 years as a board member, served as Chairperson for 3 years. Also served on the Executive and Audit Committees.

2009 to 2014 Awards Committee Member for New Mexico Association of Community College Trustees.

2008 to 2011 Commissioner, Indian Arts and Crafts Board. Completed a three-year term after being appointed by the U.S. Secretary of the Interior. He served as Vice Chair. The Commissioners supervise implementation of appropriate Bureau of Indian Affairs policies and advised the Secretary of the Interior on Native American cultural matters.

2004-2005 Selected by the American Indian Higher Education Consortium for the Kellogg Leadership Fellow for Minority Serving Institutions.

1998 to 2002 Served as Board Member, National Indian Education Association (NIEA). Chaired the Education Technology Committee. NIEA is concern with and is very active in advocating for quality educational services for Indian students, parents, and educators.

1984 to 2000 Advisory member, the American Indian Rehabilitation Research and Training Center at Northern Arizona University. Advised and assisted the Center in identifying research topics and providing training/staff development activities for tribal/state VR agencies to improve service delivery to American Indian people with special needs.

1986 to 1999 A State Committee member (vice-president) of the Navajo North Central Association (NCA). The Navajo NCA is chartered equivalent to a State by the North Central Association of Schools and Colleges. The number of NCA accredited Navajo schools has grown from twenty-six to seventy-eight since its inception in 1986.

1998 to 1999 Member of the Diné College Board of Regents. Represented the Navajo Nation President. Advised the college president and provided policy direction for the college.

1988 to 1992 Advisory member to the New Mexico State Division of Vocational Rehabilitation. Advised the agency in provision of vocational rehabilitation services to disabled citizens in the state of New Mexico.

1998 to 1999 Goals 2000 Panel Member. Represented the Navajo Nation as a Panel member to Goals 2000. Reviewed Bureau of Indian Affairs funded schools, provided grants and professional development activities to improve the academic achievements levels of Indian students.

1990 to 1991 President of the American Indian Vocational Directors Association. This association was the lobbying arm for Indian VR Projects. Presented testimony to strengthen the role of Indian tribes in provision of VR services during the reauthorization of the Rehabilitation Act. This association is now known as the Consortia of Administrators for Native American Rehabilitation (CANAR).

In addition to these activities, Dr. Guy has given PowerPoint presentations and speeches throughout the Navajo Nation, nationally, and internationally about higher education and how he sees education is important to building the future of both Navajo and the United States as a whole. He has traveled to different countries, studying their educational models and providing insights into American Indian education and the Navajo people to a wide range of audiences.

Summary

As the President of Navajo Technical University, Dr. Elmer Guy is one of the most important leaders in higher education in the United States. As a young boy, he learned about responsibility and hard work by herding sheep for his grandparents. In school he became a runner-up state champion wrestler even if he was not the most gifted of student athletes and did well enough academically to be admitted to Northern Arizona University. After struggling in higher education, he took a job as a teacher's aide in a school dedicated to serving handicapped children and young people and then went on to earn his baccalaureate degree in Vocational Rehabilitation in Special Education from the University of Arizona. Then he started as a special education teacher at the school where he had been a teacher's aide and ended up as the Executive Director of Education for the Navajo Nation. After that was over, he started his career as a college administration, becoming, not long after he started that career, a TCU President.

The key to Elmer Guy's career has been the combination of his intelligence melded to a demeanor that is always calm, deliberate, and visionary. He is a consummate politician in the sense that he has the patience to work through any political challenge, reaching consensus within a broad range of political opinions and postures, and coming up with a successful result that serves what he intends to achieve. His leadership of Navajo Technical University has built one of the most prestigious minority-serving universities in the United States. The foundation he has built for a visionary future is so strong that it promises to bring benefits not only to the Navajo people but also to American Indian people, international indigenous people, and the American nation itself.

•   C H A P T E R   3   •

The Extraordinary NTU Educational Model

The history of NTU explains some of its foundations. The current curriculum and its operations tell another part of the story. The university remains, as was true when it was the Navajo Skill Center, driven by the effort the Navajo Nation originally charged it to work toward, accomplishing, developing the knowledge, skills, attributes, and values of the Navajo work-force necessary for the Nation's economic well-being. The reason the university has such an unusual infrastructure, unlike most of the higher education systems in the U.S., is that it is charged with not only educating students but also helping to develop employment opportunities for those students in the Navajo Nation and surrounding communities. This means that the job-training and economic development mission of NTU is as important as the education mission, which helps to explain the career ladders, from micro-credentials dedicated to vocational jobs to doctoral degrees, that are still being constructed.

In addition to the career ladder design of the university, other elements are equally important. When Elmer Guy was first hired by the CIT Board of Directors as President, he made the decision to start concentrating on developing new degrees in STEM fields. The feeling of Dr. Guy and his education leadership at the time was that the American economy's future, as well as that of the world economy, would be centered in the continual changes brought about by new technologies. Most of these technologies were coming out of STEM fields, including those in health, technology, vocational/technical fields, and other areas where employment was likely to expand into the foreseeable future.

As CIT became a college and then a university, the administration also worked to get the faculty to adopt an experiential approach to education. The trades fields had always worked at teaching students by combining classroom work with projects that took place in labs or in surrounding Navajo communities. Carpentry students had repaired homes, or even built homes, for veterans or others who were deserving in the Navajo Nation. The Culinary Arts program ran the cafeteria on campus. At one point, the students served banquets to dignitaries at the Salt Lake Winter Olympics. Now NTU wanted STEM course instructors to do the same thing. Knowledge would be acquired in the classroom and then applied through projects done in either the classroom or the community as either service or research projects.

Building a Research University

A special emphasis was put upon research at the undergraduate level with the idea that, as NTU developed graduate degrees, it would have in place the foundations to become a research university that could provide intellectual property as well as high skill/high wage Diné professionals to the Navajo Nation and the Nation's families. Intellectual property, copyrights, trademarks, and patents realized through student and faculty research, was especially important in this push since such property is the foundation for much of the economic growth in areas like the Silicon Valley in California or the North Carolina Research Triangle.

As all of this was put into place, NTU also started developing laboratories, achieved mostly because of National Aeronautics and Space Administration (NASA) and NSF grants originally. Over time labs such as the Center for Advanced Manufacturing in Crownpoint or the Chemistry and Biology labs in both Crownpoint and Chinle, were built into worldclass facilities. This was designed to eventually realize the creation of entrepreneurial and new industry economic development in partnership with the Navajo Nation.

One of the unusual steps taken in the operation of NTU labs has been a process in which undergraduate students, even freshmen, are taught how to use machinery and instruments only graduate students are allowed to touch in other major universities. The idea is to make engineering or Advanced Manufacturing students, as an example, proficient, from their earliest educational experiences, in the practical side of science and processes that lead to cutting-edge research and the evolvement of scientific knowledge.

The Center for Advanced Manufacturing

Developing the Center for Advanced Manufacturing and research projects led to an increasing number of partnerships with private sector businesses, other universities, national laboratories like Sandia National Laboratories in Albuquerque, and other researchers and groups from around the United States. Following the lead of the Center, other laboratories and programs at NTU began developing similar partnerships. The extent of these partnerships involving cutting edge work in fields such as Engineering, Environmental Science, Chemistry, and Biology at NTU is truly extraordinary.

Harold (Scott) Halliday, the Director of the Center, early on learned how to "leg" into an evolving vision that has seen it become one of the most important Advanced Manufacturing and Metrology centers among the nation's colleges and universities. He has continually pushed the envelope of the center, developed grant proposals that would achieve some slice of the vision he was working toward, and then come up with funding to build another slice until he has "legged" into what once seemed unlikely if not impossible.

The NTU Veterinary Hospital and Educational Programs

However, even when NTU was CIT, long before the Center for Advanced Manufacturing was created, a veterinary technician training program was established. Navajo has embraced the herding of sheep, cattle, and horses as a central part of Navajo culture for centuries. Important cultural protocols have evolved because of the Diné herding traditions. Developing a program that trained students to care for animals made a lot of sense because the tradition is so strongly ingrained in the tribe. As part of the training program, a veterinarian clinic was developed so that students could get real world experience both operating a viable clinic business and treating both small and large animals.

The Navajo Technical University Veterinarian Hospital has been operating successfully, training students and treating animals, for decades. In addition to its veterinary technical associate degree program, it also has an Animal Sciences baccalaureate degree, an extension program that is part of NTU's land grant status, and an active research program. The hospital first introduced llamas as guard animals, has done research in several diseases that affect sheep, introduced breeding stock for both sheep and cattle herds, conducted research designed to find solutions to the domestic dogs that have gone wild, forming packs throughout the Navajo Reservation, and other projects designed to help Navajo farmers and ranchers succeed.

Other Research/Educational Projects

Currently NTU is doing Artificial Intelligence (AI) research, research in water filtration for community, livestock, and farming wells, research in battery technologies, and several other areas, often applying that research for the benefit of the Navajo Nation. The university is also exploring how waste from abandoned uranium mines can be mined to extract actinium-225 while achieving remediation at abandoned uranium mining sites that have created disastrous health outcomes for so many Navajo families. The decay properties of actinium-225 are favorable for use in targeted alpha therapy (TAT). Clinical trials have demonstrated the applicability of radiopharmaceuticals containing 225Ac to treat various types of cancer. Currently one gram is worth around three million dollars.

A good example of the research being done is the work by students and faculty in the Environmental Science and Environmental Engineering departments. The ongoing

Sustainable Water Infrastructure Project, developed through a partnership with New Mexico Technical University and a private industry partner, Process Equipment and Service Company, Inc., "relies on innovative desalination units that filter water through hollow-fiber membranes." Currently the project is focusing on providing safe water for livestock management and irrigation.

This phase will be followed by ensuring drinkable water for human consumption. Pilot models will also be introduced to high schools, showcasing the technology's functionality and potential mobility. Maintenance of these units will be undertaken by students from the community, ensuring sustainability and local involvement. Other community members will be trained on maintenance as well.[16]

The NSF Nexus Prize

Another project underway is designed to increase Energy and Food Sovereignty in Navajo by demonstrating sustainable and ecological principles on the Crownpoint campus. Led by Dr. RoyChowdhury and several Environmental students, the project is designed to integrate traditional Navajo ecological knowledge, modern sustainable technologies, and community education. Part of the project is to employ traditional Navajo farming methods, the harvesting of rainwater, and a solar-powered irrigation system to enhance the campus-based garden. The project recently was named the Phase I Winner in the U.S. Department of Energy American-Made TCU Energy and Food Sovereignty Nexus Prize.

Supporting Students

Supporting students in all the aspects of the university experience is an aggressive effort to provide programs that inspire and support efforts to earn certificates or degrees. Academic Advisement, Accommodation Services, the Bookstore, Career Services, Childcare Services, First Year Experience, the Substance Abuse and Prevention Program, Student Activities, Student Residential Services, the *Nitsáhákees Bee'anooséél* Student Success Center, the Wellness Center, and Student Athletics, are available to any NTU student. A special emphasis is placed on improving retention and graduation rates. NTU, in partnership with the federal government, Arizona and New Mexico state governments, the American Indian College Fund, and the Navajo Nation also works hard to provide as many scholarships as possible to students. Research conducted by the university over the years has established that "money problems" is one of the major reasons students fail to complete their degree programs.

Competitions

Part of both the learning and student support design are student competitions. Since the heart of the TCU movement has always been an effort to strengthen students' positive self-concepts, competitions, added to opportunities to showcase student classroom and research accomplishments, allow students to demonstrate not only their individual accomplishments but also the quality of NTU. The 2023-24 school year student accomplishments illustrate the strength and importance of this aspect of the NTU model.

NTU's 11th Annual Research Competition was held on February 29, 2024

Award Recipients

1st Place - Merrill Benally – Environmental Science - Using Atmospheric Pressure and Relative Humidity to Produce Water

2nd Place - Milton James - Energy Systems - Using Typical Meteorological /Yearly Data to Design a 700W, 24V Electrical Bike Charging Station.

3rd Place - Makeiyla Begay - Chemistry - Bending Dielectric Elastomer Actuators

3rd Place - Layla James - Biology - Assays for Rapid Detection of SARS-COV2 Infection in a Broad Spectrum of Animals

SkillsUSA

The 2024 SkillsUSA New Mexico State Leadership and Skills Conference (SLSC) was held on April 11-13, 2024, in Albuquerque. NTU students earned four (4) gold medals in electrical construction, restaurant service, digital cinema production, baking and pastry; one (1) silver medal in electrical construction wiring; and four (4) bronze medals in carpentry, electrical construction wiring, customer service, job interview, and welded sculpture.

The 2024 SkillsUSA National Competition was held from June 24–28 at the Georgia World Congress Center in Atlanta, Georgia. Angel Joe brought home the bronze medal in Restaurant Service. She practiced with Lorena Geisbrecht for this National competition.

AIHEC Annual Student Competitions

NTU Award Recipients for AIHEC Annual Conference held in Minneapolis on March 9-12, 2024:

Archery
3rd place, men's team
1st place, men's singles
2nd place, women's team
2nd place, women's singles
Art Exhibition
2nd place in painting
Basketball
3rd place, women's team
Business Bowl
3rd place in Business Bowl
Creative Writing
Best nonfiction
Cybersecurity
3rd place in cybersecurity
One Act Play
3rd place in One Act Play
Scientific Oral
2nd place in scientific oral
Scientific Poster
2nd place in scientific poster
5K Run
5th place in a 5K run, men's team
2nd place in the 5K run, men's team

E-Learning at NTU

The university also boasts a strong E-Learning capability. Currently students can earn fifteen degrees online, ranging from baccalaureate to master's degree to PhD. The infrastructure for online education at NTU masterminded by Coleen Arviso is world class, and the university is recognized for its distance education by several organizations:

Online Learning Consortium (OLC)

Navajo Technical University has become institutional members of the Online Learning Consortium (OLC) formerly Sloan-C. The Online Learning Consortium is the leading professional organization devoted to advancing quality online learning providing professional development, instruction, best practice publications and guidance to educators, online learning professionals and organizations around the world.

State Authorization Reciprocity Agreement (SARA)

Navajo Technical University (NTU) was approved as of June 7, 2017, by the New Mexico Higher Education Department (NMHED) to participate in the National Council for State Authorization Reciprocity Agreements (NC-SARA). It is the first tribal university/college to become a member of SARA. As a participating institution, NTU Online Courses/Programs are committed to follow the Interregional Guidelines for the Evaluation of Distance Education programs.

Higher Learning Commission

NTU follows the Guidelines for the Evaluation of Distance Education (Online Learning): The Guidelines have been developed by the Council of Regional Accrediting Commissions (C-RAC) to assist institutions in planning distance education and to provide an assessment framework for institutions already involved in distance education and for evaluation teams.

Western Interstate Commission for Higher Education (WIHCHE) Online Course Exchange

NTU is partners with WIHCHE Online Course Exchange. The Online Course Exchange increases access for students utilizing institutional resources more effectively. The OCE Catalog lists online courses with seats available for use by other member institutions.

WCET Membership

WCETNTU has organizational membership in WCET. WCET is the leader in the practice, policy, and advocacy of technology-enhanced learning in higher education.[17]

Technology Infrastructure at NTU

When President Guy was first appointed as President of CIT, it was, like the rest of the Navajo Nation, part of the digital divide. The Internet connectivity that existed was based on modems and telephone lines. Through a series of innovative efforts by IT staff and faculty, this challenge was tackled by building, first, the Internet to the Hogan Project that brought the first high speed connectivity to the campus using wireless connectivity sent over 120 miles from the University of New Mexico gigaPOP in Albuquerque to the Crownpoint campus. Then a classroom was established that linked 25 minicomputers together to create a high-performance computer cluster that also was used by IT students in their studies. Then projects like building a data visualization wall were undertaken by IT staff and students, creating the foundations for one of the more advanced technology infrastructures for an institution of higher education.

Today Navajo Technical University (NTU) operates a robust and scalable network infrastructure designed to meet the needs of its users with a focus on reliability, security, and futureproofing. Below is an overview of NTU's IT technology and services:

Network Infrastructure

High-Speed Fiber Optic Connection: NTU is connected to a 100 Gbps fiber optic backbone that links to Albuquerque, New Mexico, ensuring high-speed and reliable internet access.

Core Routers: The network's backbone is powered by two Cisco deep packet buffer routers, providing the scalability and redundancy needed for seamless connectivity.

Border Security: Palo Alto Networks' solutions secure the university's network perimeter, ensuring data security and protecting against external threats.

Building Connectivity: NTU provides a standard 10 Gbps backbone to every building on campus. More populated facilities will be upgraded to a 100 Gbps backbone shortly, eliminating bottlenecks and supporting increased local LAN and research demands.

Internal Network Design

Enterprise Network: NTU employs an enterprise-level internal network where departments and programs are isolated unless specific access is necessary. Segmentation enhances security and resource management.

Science DMZ: The university maintains a dedicated, unfiltered network for scientific research. This Science DMZ allows researchers to securely transmit large datasets to research partners worldwide without filters that might hinder performance.

Wi-Fi Services: NTU provides campus-wide Wi-Fi with the following features:

Transitioning to Wi-Fi 6E and testing Wi-Fi 7 for improved speed and capacity.

Multiple redundant wireless frequencies ensure uninterrupted connectivity.

Community Broadband Services

NTU extends broadband wireless services to surrounding communities, ensuring broader access to reliable internet.

Plans include expanding these services to additional neighboring communities.

Student Housing Connectivity

On-Campus Housing: The university upgrades Wi-Fi services in student dormitories and efficient apartments to ensure seamless connectivity.

Family Housing: Dedicated fiber optic networks are installed for student-family housing, prioritizing robust and reliable access.

IT Systems and Operating Platforms

NTU actively upgrades its systems to the latest versions of Windows, macOS, and Linux operating systems, providing users with up-to-date technology and tools.

Efforts are underway to adopt artificial intelligence (AI) solutions to improve departmental efficiency and enhance user experience from the moment they connect to the network.

Data Center Redevelopment

NTU is currently redeveloping its data center to accommodate data-intensive and research-driven needs. This includes:

Enhanced cooling systems to manage high-performance equipment.

Backup power generation to ensure uninterrupted operation.

Improved security measures to protect sensitive data and systems.

Research and Development Initiatives

The NTU IT department actively researches and develops to create viable solutions for IT technologies across all its campuses. Key initiatives include:

Developing efficient remote management of services, eliminating Border Gateway security by implementing homegrown firewalls

Advancing Solutions for Classroom AV Systems.

Exploring services built on new processor technologies such as ARM.

Providing innovative desktop solutions for constituents.   '

IT Department Goals and Tools

NTU continuously explores tools and technologies to enable its small IT team to operate more effectively and efficiently.

Investments in scalable and modular solutions ensure the network remains adaptable to future demands.

Strategic Vision for IT

NTU's IT Department's goal is to become the cornerstone of IT development, research, and standardization for the Navajo Nation and underserved communities worldwide. NTU aims to make a lasting global impact by prioritizing innovation and inclusivity.

Central to this is the gigaPOP, NTU's high-capacity network access point located at 505 Marquette in Albuquerque, the source of connectivity in New Mexico, providing unparalleled access to education and commercial peering networks and Internet2 resources. Strong ties to these networks allow the university to deliver substantially lower-cost Internet services—pennies on the dollar—while maintaining exceptional performance and reliability. As its own Internet Service Provider (ISP), NTU leverages access to a /22 IPv4 address space, ensuring robust, scalable connectivity. The university also collaborates with leading education networks, including Front Range GigaPOP, CENIC, Sun Corridor, and New Mexico state resources, empowering research, education, and innovation at every level.

Projects Supporting the Navajo Nation

There are several projects NTU is currently working on that are being done in concert with the Navajo Nation's administration.

The Murdered and Missing Indigenous Women (MMIW) Database Project

This project is aligned with the Nygren-Montoya[18] Administration's priorities in education, public safety, and health/social services by serving as a critical tool for addressing challenges faced by the Navajo Nation. The database NTU is putting into place supports educational priorities by leveraging data to improve outcomes and address systemic MMIW issues, addressing public safety, prosecution, and accountability priorities, provides insights to improve health and social services and address systemic social issues like substance abuse, mental health, domestic violence, homelessness, and health care access.

Building a Community Wireless System for Academic Use on the Navajo Nation

As part of its old Internet to the Hogan initiative, NTU is in the process of planning and implementing *community wireless systems for academic use on the Navajo Nation*. The project will deploy a tower, cellular on wheels (COWs), mono or wall mounted towers to provide interconnect between NTU and other higher education external network services for backhaul to Albuquerque, NM. The project will deploy connectivity (100GB down/20 up) in alignment with NTU's science and research needs in a community.

The intent is to enhance academic access by deploying wireless services (CBRS, EBS [in cooperation with Comnet/Sacred Wind Communications in Crownpoint], or 5.8 GHz unlicensed spectrum) where current resources are lacking, in collaboration
with higher education institutions utilizing research education network resources to adapt to evolving educational requirements.

Partnership to Address Lack of Remote Access in Rural Areas

NTU is working with Diné College and other higher education institutions to address the lack of remote access to academic programs in service area communities like Crownpoint, Littlewater, Casamero Lake, Borrego Pass, Red Mesa (Community/Crownpoint Public Safety), and the NTU Campus at Chinle. NTU intends to collaborate with Navajo ETCs to demonstrate cooperative services, where possible.

Business, Entrepreneurial Culture, and Creativity

Part of what the NTU Educational Model is working to achieve is the strengthening of foundational elements that support the strengthening of the Navajo Nation itself and economic development for both the Nation and surrounding communities in New Mexico, Arizona, and Utah. There are several elements to this effort. The first of these at NTU was to create a degree in Business Management and Hospitality and Restaurant management in support of what the Navajo Economic Development

Division perceived to be core educational programs that would strengthen their efforts. This was followed by expanding an associate degree in accounting to a baccalaureate degree and an attempt to partner with the private sector to provide internships to students pursuing administrative and/or accounting careers.

Paired with this was the effort to further the creativity-focused educational efforts at NTU, emphasizing creative writing, Navajo crafts like weaving, and new media. This creative element is bolstered by sponsoring events around creative efforts by students and other Navajo writers, artists, and craftspeople on campus, often with a cultural element, that attracts students from engineering, technology, and other fields. The idea is that if you create a creative cultural environment on campus, the environment will help spark creative efforts in unexpected places.

The Navajo people have long had a history of creativity and entrepreneurism. At NTU, vendors of breakfast sandwiches or Navajo arts and crafts set up shop every day to market their wares and creations at different places on campus. Throughout both Navajo and Zuni there are shops that market arts and crafts, and roadside food stands, and craft markets are set up. One of the goals of Navajo Tech is to harness this creativity and entrepreneurial drive through its curriculum and then develop linkages between that creativity, management, entrepreneurism, and even STEM programs, giving Navajo the ability to become an economic leader in the 21st century.

Navajo Technical University Innovation Center

Part of the effort to create synergy between creativity, entrepreneurism, and business has been the development of the Navajo Technical University Innovation Center near Church Rock, New Mexico. A partnership with the Navajo Economic Development Division, the center has a conference area where workshops and other educational activities can occur as well as incubator space for Navajo entrepreneurs in the process of starting their own businesses. The Center has been filled with entrepreneurs since its opening and exists as an integral link between educational programming and the extension of that programming into practical efforts to strengthen the Navajo economy. NTU extends its research and educational efforts out of the classroom to serve the entire Navajo Nation.

The Hole in Economic Development Efforts by Universities in the United States

All of this does not fully cover all the educational model developed at NTU, though. A lot of work is done by the various academic departments with different divisions within the Navajo Nation to explore where the Nation wants to drive progress. One of the most important goals of the Nation has long been to develop economic development for the benefit of the Navajo people.

One of the biggest holes in economic development efforts in the United States exists when efforts are made to transfer work accomplished in university laboratories into the private sector. Through the NSF, NASA, the Department of Energy, the Nuclear Regulatory Commission, and Department of Defense Research labs, and other agencies, universities can apply and receive funding for research projects. Then, in the usual economic development model for projects with business possibilities, venture-capital firms fund start-ups, or an outside corporation comes in and sets up a production or business facility.

The hole in economic development in poor communities occurs when the volume of production and sales potential required for venture capital funding is not possible for small universities like NTU to access. Either the infrastructure to develop a business is not available in tribal communities to achieve the volumes of production necessary to achieve funding, or the university does not have the number of personnel to ramp up to that production level, or there is a difficulty in proving the project in a way attractive to venture capital firms or outside corporations. This is exasperated, inevitably, by the reluctance of capital to invest in geographic areas with a history of poverty.

Most of the new jobs created in the United States are created by small business, so there is a hole that exists in economic development in this country. This hole exists in the need for funding that allows the development of proof-of-concept and pilot projects designed to generate income based upon research that does not demand volumes of sales, or the location, required by venture capitalists.

The Development of Iíná LLC

The Board of Regents this year set up Iíná LLC, a holding company that NTU owns, as a profit-making company. Any excess profits will be used to either forward economic development efforts by NTU for the Navajo people or to support the university's mission. The first major initiative of Iíná put into place uses the work of the Center for Advanced Manufacturing and a range of partnership initiatives with Sandia National Laboratories, Arizona State University, federal agencies, the State of New Mexico, and private sector firms. This work has resulted in the creation of products that can meet significant demands in the national marketplace while unlocking untapped creativity from around the Navajo Nation. Navajo Advanced Manufacturing Enterprise (NAME) is the first development of Iíná, although other enterprise developments are anticipated in the future.

This effort ties into other efforts at the Center of Advance Manufacturing in workforce education, research in processes, and even into the use of Artificial Intelligence (AI) in products and materials created by Advanced Manufacturing (AM) machining. Partnerships with New Mexico State University and Purdue University where Navajo graduate degree students are using a combination of online education and the tools and equipment located in the Center in Crownpoint to earn their graduate degrees, and of course NTU's extensive engineering, Advanced Manufacturing, and business degree programs, are part of the economic development effort intended to form the intellectual backbone of cutting-edge business development for the Navajo people.

At its heart, Iíná is designed to provide a working model that addresses the hole in U.S. economic development created by the lack of funding for projects that fall between venture capitalist or corporate requirements for business development and what university research labs have created. At the same time, high wage, high skill jobs filled by NTU graduates will help Navajo families and the Navajo Nation's overall economic development efforts.

Capstone Courses

Supporting Iíná and other development efforts is the capstone course design. In capstone courses, NTU encourages faculty to work with small teams of senior students that partner with the university's economic development effort, private sector businesses, or through service projects to create new products or services of value to the business or community involved but that are not being pursued. These teams are often multi-disciplinary in nature, involving students working toward different degrees.

An early example of this effort was when Culinary Arts students partnered with students from the Alternative Energy program to create solar ovens useful to Navajo living in areas with limited power resources and little money. These projects can come from any education department in the university; however, especially from the ABET accredited programs in collaboration with the Business degree programs.

The hope is that individual students involved in capstone courses will take an entrepreneurial leap and work toward the creation of a Navajo business that hires Navajo workers, possibly working with the NTU Innovation Center. There is also a hope that a capstone project will be licensed by a private sector firm or funded as a community service, again creating jobs in Navajo communities.

• C H A P T E R 4 •

Summary of the NTU Higher Education Model

Conveying the vision that drives the NTU Higher Education Model is challenging. The challenge lies in the model's complexity. When Dr. Elmer Guy became President of CIT, he brought with him an idea that in large part emerged from an AIHEC event called the Circle of Prosperity held in Silicon Valley in 1999. At the time, the digital divide was especially severe in Native Nations. The idea behind the event was to come up with strategies that could be implemented by the tribal colleges to "bridge" the divide and make Native communities and people more competitive in the U.S. and global marketplace. Over one hundred representatives from tribal, federal and state governments, Tribal Colleges and other higher education institutions, the private sector, and non-profit organizations convened in Palo Alto, CA for three days of exploration, brainstorming, and problem-solving, focusing on collaborative solutions to the digital divide across Indian Country.[19]

One of the concepts emerging out of that meeting was that new wealth tends to be created at the edges of technology. Technology in this sense refers not just to computers and systems like the Internet. Means of generating fire at one point in human history represented a cutting-edge and transformative technology. So, from the very beginning of Dr. Guy's tenure, the idea was to build an institution of higher education that would attempt to put NTU in the engine of the technology train rather than always playing catch-up in the caboose from the rest of the world.[20] By building a world class institution within an ecosystem of partnerships and collaborations supported by new and emerging technologies, the history of poverty in the Navajo Nation could be reversed and moved toward a time of economic growth and greater prosperity.

The ecosystem built to work toward such an ambitious goal was necessarily going to be complex. Not only would the approach to teaching need to be effective with students, but expectations would have to be raised, and the curriculum built around STEM and health careers would have to be constructed so that it was both innovative and far-sighted. Just doing what every other college in the U.S. was doing wouldn't put the college on the "bleeding edge" of technology development. Academic programs would also have to be developed in a broad range of disciplines that related to the future of the Navajo Nation and its people.

Challenges in building such a college were numerous. As the Crownpoint Institute of Technology became a college and then a university, pushback against ideas like requiring higher forms of mathematics such as calculus in a field like Information Technology, then in engineering programs, came up against the idea that Indians are lousy at math, a myth quickly dispelled once students had to meet the expectations built into their programs. Instructors sometimes were afraid that more rigorous requirements would result in lower enrollments in their programs, threatening their jobs. Sometimes this was true for the short-term, reducing enrollment in a program after standards were strengthened. But Dr. Guy kept pushing and pushing, slowly building the ecosystem originally envisioned. After a semester or two, the newly constituted programs that had lost enrollment regained their enrollment when expectations students had about the program's rigor had changed.

Simply an outline of the ecosystem created and now in place at NTU can look somewhat daunting:

Graphic Environmental Model Components

1. **Historical Context**:
   - Origin from the Navajo Skills Center in 1969.
   - Response to high unemployment and poverty within the Navajo Nation.
   - Operation as a tribal college, leading to becoming a university.
2. **Educational Framework**:
   - Career ladder structure (micro-credentials to PhD).
   - Emphasis on vocational/technical education alongside STEM programs.
   - Integration of Diné culture, language, and experiential learning.
3. **Economic Development Goals**:
   - Direct alignment with the economic needs of the Navajo Nation.
   - Creation of job opportunities through training and education.

- o Development of Iíná LLC to fill gap in economic development.
- o Capstone courses developed in partnership with the private sector, the Navajo Nation, and national laboratories

4. **Research and Innovation:**
   - o Focus on undergraduate research and partnerships with national laboratories, universities.
   - o Development of advanced manufacturing, veterinary, chemistry, environmental, biology, etc. programs.
   - o Projects addressing local needs (e.g., water filtration, MMIW database).

5. **Community Engagement:**
   - o Service projects and partnerships with local chapterhouses, businesses.
   - o Hands-on learning through community-based initiatives, capstone projects.
   - o Building a wireless system for academic use in the Navajo Nation.

6. **Support Systems:**
   - o Comprehensive student support services.
   - o Collaborations with federal and state organizations for scholarships and funding.

7. **Technology Infrastructure:**
   - o Robust IT systems and broadband initiatives to bridge the digital divide.
   - o Research DMZ with other universities and national laboratories
   - o E-learning capabilities to increase access to education.

8. **Creativity and Entrepreneurial Culture**:
   - ○ Encouragement of creative programs and businesses.
   - ○ Creation of "creative environment" on campuses and instructional sites.
   - ○ Innovation Center to support local entrepreneurs.

Relationships and Interactions

Feedback Loops: Between education, research, the private sector, national laboratories and other universities, and community projects to adapt and evolve based on local needs and outcomes.

Partnerships: Collaboration with other institutions, businesses, and government agencies for resource sharing and economic growth.

Cultural Integration: Ensuring that Diné culture is interwoven in all programs and initiatives, fostering identity and community pride.

Graphic Representation of Outline

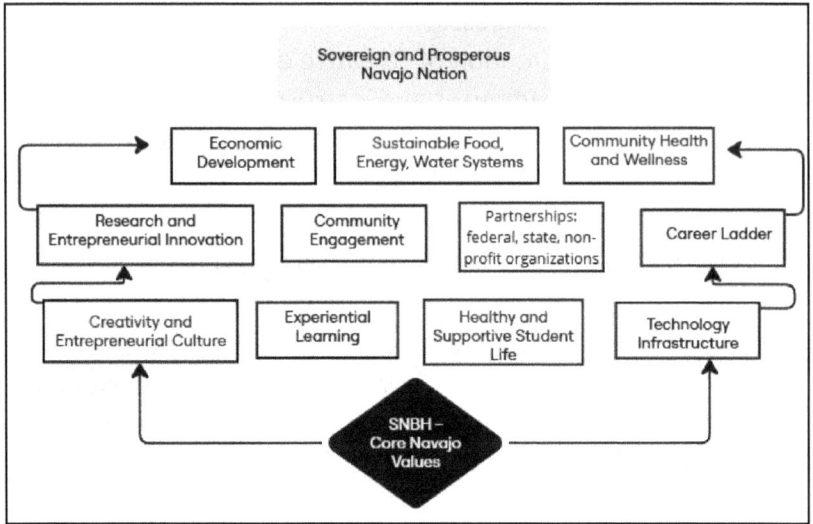

Summary

Navajo Technical University is breaking new ground with its extraordinary higher education model. The model starts out with a career ladder approach that emphasizes vocational/technical trades areas of studies and runs through the various degree levels to PhD programs. Throughout all these ladders that have been created, there is an emphasis upon Diné culture and language, experiential models of education, creativity as a strong Navajo attribute, and cutting-edge research conducted by students and faculty. There is also an emphasis upon cross-disciplinary projects and projects that serve communities and work toward achieving goals and objectives set by the Navajo Nation. Often, as was the case with the development of the Bachelor of Applied Science degree in Hotel and Restaurant Management, entire degree or certificate programs are created at the request of a division or department of the Navajo Nation.

The entire curriculum and projects are aimed at serving students and the Diné and Zuni people and creating economic development and encouraging creativity. This has led to many partnerships with other colleges and universities, federal agencies, the state governments in New Mexico and Arizona, federal agencies, and both large and small businesses and corporations in the private sector.

From its beginning as part of the tribal colleges and universities movement, to its melding of trades and academic education through designed career ladders emphasizing experiential teaching models leading to research and community service projects designed to create intellectual property or benefits for the Navajo people, NTU has been creating a creative engine designed to help one of the poorest areas in the United States to excel during the 21st century.

There is not another educational model like NTU in the United States, and the truth is that its extraordinary work is only beginning.

● C H A P T E R 5 ●

The Future

Dual Credit and Student Services

Although NTU has provided dual enrollment courses in partnership with high schools in New Mexico and Arizona for over a decade now, this initiative is continuing to be a key strategy used to address the future of higher education inside the Navajo Nation. Students earning NTU credits while in high school can transfer their credits to other colleges and universities, and often do, but Navajo Tech is using this strategy to not only attract Navajo students to NTU but also to help high schools improve their performance, encouraging students to attend post-secondary education.

This strategy does not automatically provide a direct benefit to NTU in the form of increased enrollment. Some of the university's supporters sometimes criticize the dual credit program on that basis. But the strategy is designed to help all Navajo, addressing the mission given to NTU by the tribal legislature. The thinking has been, from the beginning of the effort, that by increasing the numbers of students enrolling in colleges and universities, NTU would benefit both directly through some increased enrollment and indirectly through greater support for higher education throughout the Navajo Nation as the tribal citizenship becomes increasingly educated and willing to invest tribal resources in higher education. Through the dual credit program, several students have earned their associate degree on the same day they earned their high school diploma.

In the past, 80% of NTU enrollees had one to three basic skill deficiencies. This statistic has shown some improvement since the implementation of the dual credit program. A lot of work still needs to be done with schools enrolling significant numbers of Navajo students, but one statistic showing an upward trend is that the number of young students entering NTU has shown a significant upswing. The average age of the student population is falling, at least partially due to the Dual Credit effort.

The dual credit program is paired with Student Services programs designed to improve retention and graduation rates. This is a major focus for the future. Navajo Tech, like other TCUs, have struggled with these rates. They do better than mainstream universities in retaining Indian students and graduating them overall, but their rates have always lagged general higher education student populations. NTU, through efforts like the First Year Student project, which provides advanced academic work for students who have graduated from high school the summer before enrollment and special support during the student's first year, has made gains in retention and graduation rates.

The effort to develop retention and graduation programs will not only continue in the future, but more programs are planned. The goal is to continue to improve until NTU is at least equal in these rates to other colleges and universities in its service area.

Expansion of and Changes to Instructional Sites

Currently Navajo Tech operates the main campus in Crownpoint and instructional sites in Chinle and Teec Nos Pos, the small site in Kirtland in partnership with Central Consolidated School District, and another site on the Zuni Nation. Several efforts are underway to change the campus and instructional site profile of the university:

Make the Chinle Instructional Site a Full Campus

Plans are underway to secure Higher Learning Commission approval to change the status of the Chinle Instructional site into a full campus. The Chinle Instructional Site is the oldest of NTU's instructional sites and has by far the largest enrollment. It also has a full, robust curriculum and a beautiful campus located in the heart of the Navajo Nation. Changing the accreditation status of Chinle to that of a full campus would strengthen the site and lead to an increased enrollment in one of the most populated centers of the Navajo.

The Dream of a Navajo Medical School Near Window Rock

One of NTU's goals is the effort to open an additional instructional site in Ft. Defiance focused on allied health fields. The *Tsehootsoi* Medical Facility is located less than two miles from land donated to NTU by the Window Rock School District adjacent to Window Rock High School on the New Mexico side of the New Mexico/Arizona border. Official transfer of the site from the school district to the university from the Navajo Nation is still needed. However, preliminary planning for the infrastructure needed before higher education programs can be located at the site is underway. Development of a partnership with the hospital will also be needed to support quality development of allied health programs. Micro credentials in allied health are being developed and can be easily offered out of the new site when completed.

Navajo leaders have, since the 1970s, had the dream of establishing a medical college dedicated to Indian health challenges. NTU has a pre-med program currently that has seen students enroll in different medical schools around the United States. If the Fort Defiance facility is built, funds will be sought to establish a medical college in partnership with the medical school at another university, following the model of some of the rural medical college programs like the one started by the University of Kansas.

This model envisions a partnership between the Navajo medical college (preliminary discussions have been held with the University of Arizona) with an established institution that can provide part of the coursework through distance education to the Window Rock campus. Students would be able to transfer from the pre-med program currently in place at NTU into the college near Window Rock. Most of the classes would be held at the Navajo campus. A partnership would be put into place with *Tsehootsoi* Medical facility in Ft. Defiance, and internships and some classes for medical students would be held there.

On the Crownpoint campus, the effort to strengthen pre-med programming and the Registered Nursing program are both related to the dream of eventually being able to create the Navajo Medical College. In the end, since the medical college would be aimed at health concerns that affect American Indians nationwide, the college would seek to serve all tribal nations across the United States.

Merging Instructional Sites

Another ongoing discussion involves combining the Teec Nos Pos, AZ and Kirtland, NM instructional sites into one larger site in Shiprock, NM that serves the entire region. Discussion is pending based on a family who is interested in donating land to NTU. When the new campus site is completed, current site coordinators will remain focused on their service areas but will have a facility designed to meet their respective growing student populations. Funding to create a "Northern Navajo Instructional Site" will need to be secured to make this a reality.

Plans for the Zuni Instructional Site

When NTU agreed to open an instructional site with the Zuni Nation after the University of New Mexico decided to close their operations on Zuni, the university also agreed to assist Zuni with the creation of their own tribal college under the Tribal Colleges and Universities Act federal legislation under which most of the TCUs operate. As part of the support to the formation of A:shiwi College, NTU has been exploring how to strengthen our relationship with Zuni, especially through the construction of career ladders in partnership with A:shiwi that encourage students to enroll in more advanced programs at NTU, while ensuring the new Zuni TCU gains acceptance as an institution of higher learning.

Curriculum Development in the Engine of the Technology Train, AI, Cybersecurity, and Engineering

Artificial Intelligence

Navajo Tech is continuing its effort to drive the engine rather than remain in the caboose of the technology train making transformative changes throughout the world. One of its most urgent projects has to do with Artificial Intelligence (AI). The university has been working with AI for some time now. In the finance department, NTU administrators and staff from the department have been working with Harshwal & Company, LLC, long-term consultants to the university, to install and test systems that utilize AI, robotics, and advanced analytics to improve the department's efficiency and especially provide support services to grant directors and PIs.

Even more advanced work has been ongoing with the Center for Advanced Manufacturing where a partnership between Navajo Tech and a manufacturer of Metal AM machines, Ridgeline Manufacturing, focuses on using AI to improve the ability of an advanced form of the AM machine that effectively calibrates the performance of a wide range of metal composites designed with specific requirements, especially for the aerospace and space industries

The Center has also been working with Santa Fe Community College to develop an AI enabled learning system designed to train technicians in the use of advanced instrumentation and machinery used by manufacturers involved in Advanced Manufacturing. A severe shortage of these technicians exists in the U.S. This project is especially aimed at workforce development so that micro-credentials and one-year certificate programs can lead to immediate high skill, high wage jobs.

On deck now are plans to create an innovative AI instructional, curriculum development, and laboratory project. The university plans to hire an AI assistant professor that will teach parttime in NTU's Computer Science and Information Technology ABET accredited degree programs while spending the remaining time working with professors and staff in the Advanced Manufacturing, Electrical Engineering, Environmental Science, and Chemistry labs, helping to advance research in those fields. In addition, NTU is working with other TCUs from around the nation to further AI programs in those schools, hoping to expand the effectiveness of AI education to Native populations throughout the United States.

Cybersecurity

Three years ago, working with private industry partners and the Department of Defense, NTU launched an associate degree in cybersecurity. Work is continuing to strengthen enrollment in this degree program, but, as the program develops, the plan is to build it into a baccalaureate degree. Collaboration between the AI lab being created and the cybersecurity faculty to keep up with all the development expected in cybersecurity as threats grow in sophistication with AI being used to penetrate networks and security systems. This is paired with the AI cybersecurity work described earlier that is being pursued by NTU's IT department.

Engineering

Currently NTU is the only tribal university that has achieved ABET accreditation for its engineering programs. The university offers baccalaureate degrees in Electrical

Engineering, Mechanical Engineering, Environmental Engineering, Industrial Engineering, and Advanced Manufacturing Engineering Technology. NTU engineering faculty are developing a PhD program in Electrical Engineering to be launched in 2026.

One of the big controversies in Washington DC involves the push by major businesspeople to increase the number of engineers in the United States through legal immigration. There is a severe shortage of creative, highly skilled engineers in the country, and China is outpacing the U.S. in the education of engineers, especially those trained in more advanced technologies.[21]

There are significantly fewer Native American engineers in the U.S. (as a percentage of their respective populations) than those from any other racial or ethnic group. Navajo Tech is helping to address this gap, graduating a class of Native American engineers that are creative and highly skilled, possessing advanced technology skills, every year.

NTU has a need for a more advanced building constructed specifically for experiential engineering education. Finding the funding for any kind of building is difficult for all the TCUs. Navajo Tech has been more successful than most at securing funding for building projects. The states of New Mexico and Arizona have both helped the university increase the sophistication and size of its campuses and instructional sites.

This is a project that is on the drawing boards that will have national importance in addressing the engineering shortage currently hobbling the country's efforts to compete with China and the rest of the world's advanced countries. A new engineering building with engineering laboratories, equipment, and instrumentation will also foster an increased research, capstone courses, community services, and economic agenda that helps move forward the ambitious goals President Guy has for the university.

The Engineering Building plan envisions a two-story building, including classrooms, laboratories, and faculty offices. There will be a 10-foot hallway and wide stairways with elevators. Elevators are designed to be wide enough to handle movement of laboratory equipment and materials. The total area of the proposed building is 25,000 ft.[2]

On the first floor (12,500 Sq. ft), Civil, Mechanical, Environmental, and Industrial Engineering laboratories, due to heavy lab equipment, will be housed. On the second floor (12,500 Sq. ft), Computer, Communication, Power system, and Chemical Engineering Laboratories will be located.

The new labs will be designed, as the Advanced Manufacturing Center is currently designed, to put NTU into the forefront of both engineering education and research in the United States.

Trades

For decades, many of the highest enrollment programs at Navajo Tech have been in trades fields. The glass ceiling, especially in rural areas of the Navajo Nation, exists partially because of the unavailability of professional Navajo role models, especially in STEM fields, that students encounter in their daily lives. They do often know and may be related to electricians and carpenters and other trades people, though, and this becomes an aspiration that seems to be more in reach.

The latest trade program added into the curriculum has been Plumbing at the Bond Wilson instructional site. This joins Automotive Technology, Building Information Modeling, Chemical Engineering Technology, Construction Technology, Culinary Arts, Professional Baking, Energy

Systems, and Welding where trades certificates and associate of applied science degrees are available.

The biggest challenge facing the trades currently is that most of the programs have outgrown building space available, especially in Crownpoint. New Mexico has funded architecture and engineering for renovation and expansion of the current trades building in Crownpoint. Funding for construction of the expansion is still being put together, but this is a major priority for NTU's administration. The equipment to enhance each of the trades programs is already owned by the university.

The Chinle, Bond Wilson, and Teec Nos Pos instructional sites also offer and have space for trades programs that will be developed further in the future. If the university goes ahead and consolidates Teec Nos Pos and Kirtland sites into a larger Shiprock site, then that site will primarily be dedicated to trades programs.

Technology

As is evident in the model described earlier, NTU has had an ambitious technology agenda for a long time. The Vice President, Jason Arviso, has worked closely with the Navajo Nation as well as the IT department at the university and at other tribal colleges to continually advance the availability and sophistication of technology resources for each of these groups.

A significant project currently underway in partnership with the Navajo Nation is to construct a Health Insurance Portability and Accountability Act (HIPPA) qualified datacenter at the Crownpoint campus that can be used by law enforcement and social services. The first part of that project is a database centered around Missing and Murdered Indigenous Women, a major concern for the

Navajo Nation. After this database is up and running, extensions of the database work are planned.

Especially important are the efforts to consult with the Navajo Nation to help it achieve better, more affordable connectivity. NTU became its own Internet provider to reduce costs some time ago, but not only are there significant gaps in connectivity across the nation, where it is available it is more expensive than in communities near the Nation's borders where other provider options exist. Creating more wireless hotspots for education purposes is also a continual effort that has been ongoing since the pandemic, which hit the Navajo Nation particularly hard.

The university is also working on projects across the curriculum and in the technology and other laboratories that specifically address the use of advanced tools (like data-drive decision making) to maintain NTU's competitive edge, keeping programs aligned with workforce and economic opportunities, changes in technology, student learning outcome factors, and community priorities that ensures NTU remains an irreplaceable resource for Navajo people for generations to come and continues to be a model for all TCUs.

The Navajo Environmental Center

At the Chinle instructional site, NTU is currently in the process of establishing the Navajo Environmental Center. The Center is a project designed to achieve several important goals that Navajo Technical University (NTU) and its Environmental Science and Environmental Engineering faculty have been pursuing for several years. The work being done in Chinle is attempting to accomplish the following:

- Creating a United States Environmental Protection Agency (USEPA) certified laboratory with the capability of providing quality control for the Navajo Nation with the abandoned uranium mine cleanup currently underway through superfund funding.
- Using equipment, instrumentation, and staffing of the laboratory to market its services to other communities and tribal groups facing environmental cleanup challenges. This will help pay for the lab's long-term operations.
- Increasing the ability of NTU to conduct research related to mitigation of environmental challenges present in high desert environments, including water scarcity, the growth of sand dunes, erosion, heavy metal contamination, loss of endangered plants, insects, and animals, among other issues. Research into technologies and practices that can help the Navajo people develop intellectual property that can contribute to the Navajo Nation's economic well-being is part of the center's design.
- Utilizing the Center as a launching pad for graduate and undergraduate-level programs designed to strengthen ecological/ environmental expertise available to the Navajo Nation as it tries to strengthen environmental resiliency, especially regarding dealing with water shortages for agriculture, ranching/herding, and meeting the needs of people and businesses, the provision of sustainable energy resources, and improvement of the Navajo people's economic wellbeing.
- Participating in research partnerships with institutions like the University of Arizona, Arizona

State University, Northern Arizona University, the University of New Mexico, and New Mexico Tech designed to address dryland concerns in water and energy resiliency as well as regional economic development, fueling a cycle of innovation and economic development.

- Assembling teams of researchers, students, and industry to invent, develop and deploy solutions to the most pressing challenges identified by community partners leading to actions addressing water quality and climate change.

Research on Benefiting Economically While Cleaning Up Abandoned Uranium Mine Waste

The Center will also be the focal point for Navajo Tech's work on exploring the feasibility of mining abandoned uranium mine waste as part of the removal process from the Navajo Nation. The decay properties of actinium-225 are favorable for use in targeted alpha therapy (TAT); clinical trials have demonstrated the applicability of radiopharmaceuticals containing 225Ac to treat various types of cancer. However, the scarcity of this isotope resulting from its necessary synthesis in cyclotrons limits its potential applications. The abandoned uranium mine waste contains significant amounts of isotope used in TAT. One of the Center's tasks will be to try to translate what can be done with the waste to create economic value for the Navajo people, especially since extremely small quantities of processed waste can generate significant revenue.

Generating health benefits for cancers treatments out of the waste, given the disastrous health consequences the waste has represented to the Navajo people, would be a significant signature describing how the Diné try to always improve life as they face their challenges.

Development of the Iíná Holding Company

Iíná Enterprises has been established by Navajo Technical University as a holding company to create for-profit operating entities (enterprises) that uses intellectual property (defined as copyrights, trademarks, patents, or human resources) developed by the university or can create an operating profit in a way that benefits the university or the Navajo people through the creation of high skill, high wage jobs. Although owned by the university, Iíná is part of the private sector. It is designed to fill the hole in economic development discussed earlier.

The first major enterprise under Iíná, called Navajo Advanced Manufacturing Enterprises (NAME), is in the process of being established. Ambitious plans designed to expand the business have been developed, but the initial manufacturing facility set up will be designed to produce powder for metal AM machines that contain different combinations of metals to produce specific manufactured parts. Usually called powder manufacturing, those from NTU developing the enterprise have developed an initial customer base that has indicated they are ready to purchase the first powders produced. All the equipment required for the enterprise has been purchased and is ready to install.

The current volume of sales for Powder Manufacturing for Metal AM nationwide is estimated to be in the range of several hundred million dollars annually. As Metal AM continues to grow as a component of the overall manufacturing sector in the U.S., analysts are projecting a compound annual growth rate (CAGR) of around 15-20%.

Further advancements in technology may increase that CAGR.

Current efforts to build a small manufacturing facility in Crownpoint are underway. Efforts are also being made to secure a larger facility in Gallup, New Mexico.

Expansion plans for NAME are also in place. As soon as the powder manufacturing plant is up and running, the enterprise will start Metal Prototyping for customers, a low volume, high value operation needed by the automotive, aerospace and growing space industry. With the New Mexico Space Port growing in customers, the local space industry will need to continue to develop new parts for their applications. Again, instrumentation and equipment needed for this expansion has been ordered and is ready to install once a facility is in place.

Beyond this effort, Iíná will be developing further enterprises to take advantage of the database, datacenter, and cybersecurity work NTU has been developing for over a decade. This aspect of the company will not begin until the powder manufacturing enterprise is underway.

Navajo Technical University Statistics

The statistics of NTU show a dramatic drop in enrollment and other challenges during the three pandemic years that created so many problems for so much of American society. In the Navajo Nation, the pandemic was especially severe, causing widespread illness and death. Since the pandemic was declared ended on May 5, 2019, the Nation has continued to struggle with the illness, but enrollment has slowly started to recover. The two largest TCUs in the country have consistently been either NTU or Diné College, both located in the Navajo Nation. NTU is consistently the largest tribal university.

Over the years, retention and graduation rates have been a challenge at all NTUs. Compared to the Native American enrollments in mainstream colleges and universities, TCU rates have been comparable but still leave room for growth. Recently, programs operated by Student Services have shown promising progress in improving both rates.

Navajo Technical University Statistics

After the pandemic, the enrollment has been slowly recovering. This trend is expected to continue. The Navajo population is a young population, there are large numbers of people who dropped out of either high school or an institution of higher education, and the Navajo economy is improving at a slow but steady rate over historical norms. These factors feed into potential enrollment at NTU.

Navajo Technical University Enrollment by Semester and Headcount
Fall 2012 - Fall 2024

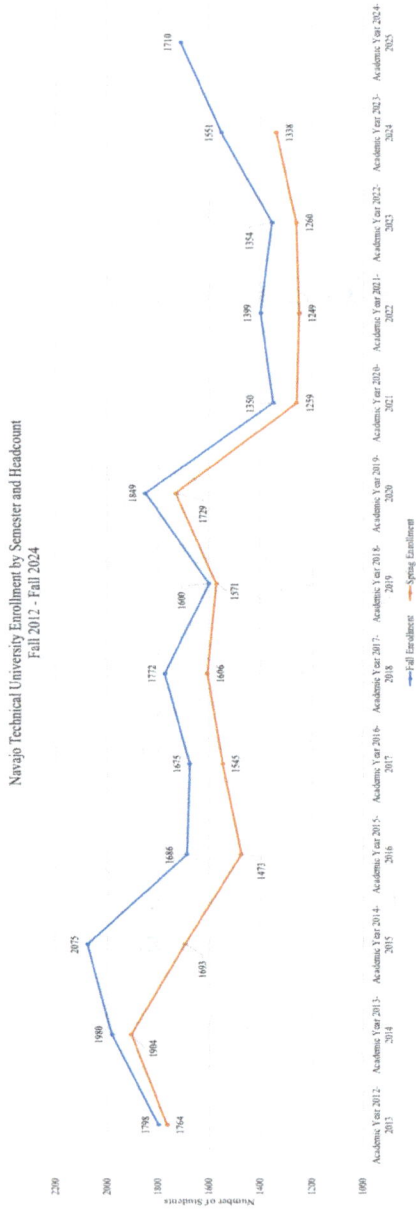

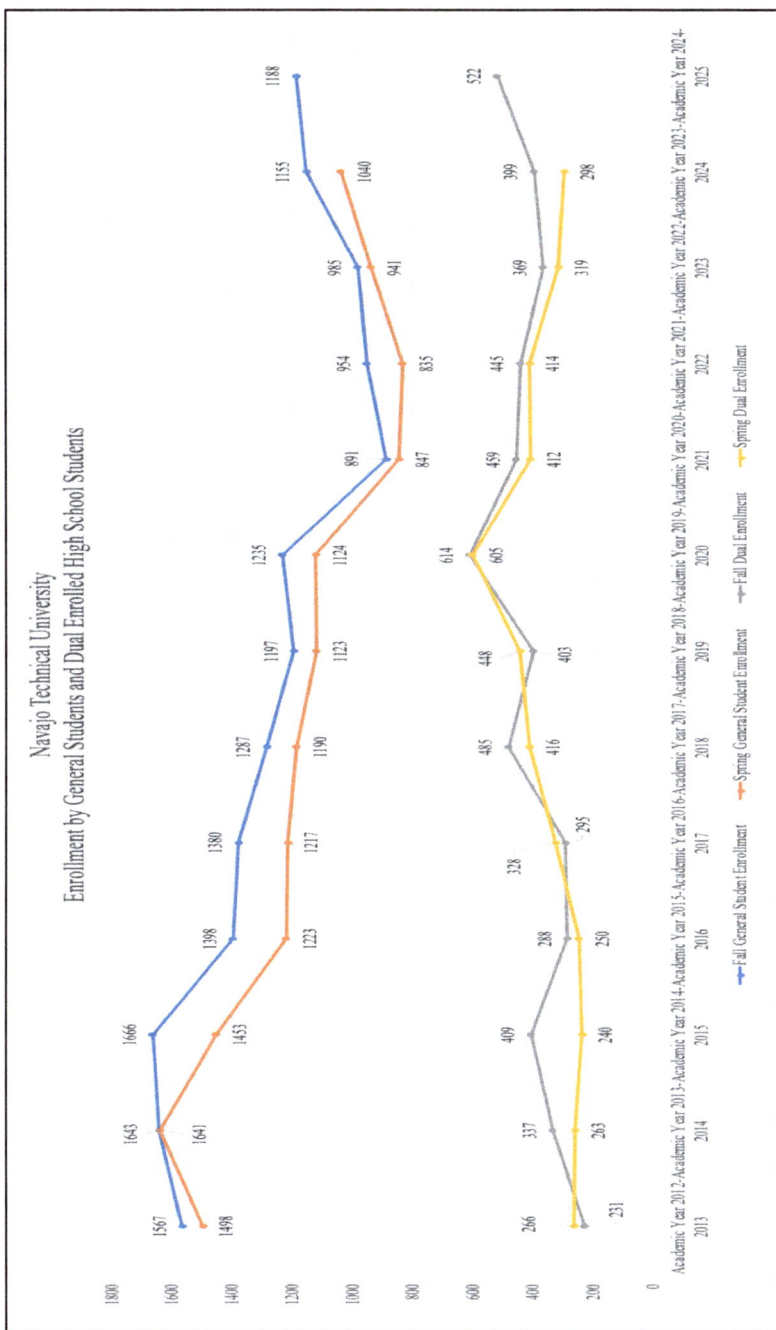

Navajo Technical University
Enrollment by General Students and Dual Enrolled High School Students

Fall General Student Enrollment — Spring General Student Enrollment — Fall Dual Enrollment — Spring Dual Enrollment

Academic Year 2012-Academic Year 2013-Academic Year 2014-Academic Year 2015-Academic Year 2016-Academic Year 2017-Academic Year 2018-Academic Year 2019-Academic Year 2020-Academic Year 2021-Academic Year 2022-Academic Year 2023-Academic Year 2024-

The dual enrollment program provides NTU credit to qualified high school students throughout the Navajo Nation in New Mexico, Arizona, and Utah. NTU is dedicated to building the Navajo community and reducing the education gap between the Navajo Nation and surrounding communities in these three states. Some of these students choose to continue their higher education at NTU, but others enroll in other colleges and universities around the United States. NTU also expects dual credit enrollment in NTU to grow over time, albeit slowly. NTU is also working with high school faculty to strengthen standards so that fewer students enter colleges and universities with basic skill deficiencies at the rates experienced in the past. The plan is to eliminate the differential in educational attainment between the Navajo Nation's population and the populations in the surrounding states.

As seen from the above chart, enrollment at NTU declined for an extended period but is now starting to grow again. The pandemic did not help, but enrollment is now close to pre-pandemic levels.

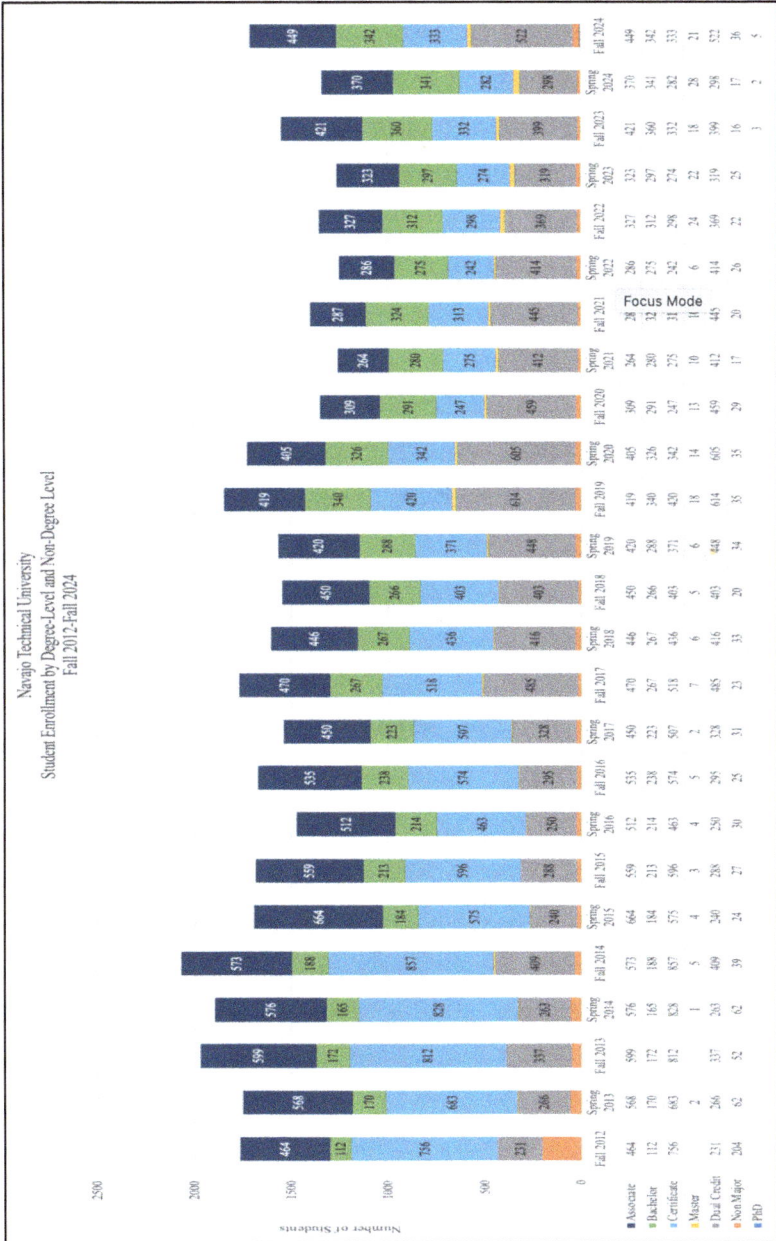

Navajo Technical University
Student Enrollment by Degree-Level and Non-Degree Level
Fall 2012-Fall 2024

Number of Students

Focus Mode

Legend: Associate, Bachelor, Certificate, Master, Dual Credit, Non Major, PhD

	Fall 2012	Spring 2013	Fall 2013	Spring 2014	Fall 2014	Spring 2015	Fall 2015	Spring 2016	Fall 2016	Spring 2017	Fall 2017	Spring 2018	Fall 2018	Spring 2019	Fall 2019	Spring 2020	Fall 2020	Spring 2021	Fall 2021	Spring 2022	Fall 2022	Spring 2023	Fall 2023	Spring 2024	Fall 2024
Associate	464	568	599	576	573	664	559	512	535	450	470	446	450	420	419	405	309	264	28	286	327	323	421	370	449
Bachelor	112	170	172	165	188	184	213	214	238	223	267	267	266	288	340	326	291	280	32	275	312	297	360	341	342
Certificate	756	683	812	828	857	575	596	463	574	507	518	436	403	371	430	342	247	275	31	242	298	274	332	282	333
Master		2		1	5	4	3	4	5	2	7	6	5	6	18	14	13	10	1	6	24	22	18	28	21
Dual Credit	231	266	337	263	409	340	288	250	295	328	485	416	403	448	614	605	459	412	445	414	369	319	399	298	522
Non Major	204	62	52	62	39	24	27	30	28	31	23	33	20	34	35	35	29	17	20	26	22	25	16	17	26
PhD																							3	2	5

135

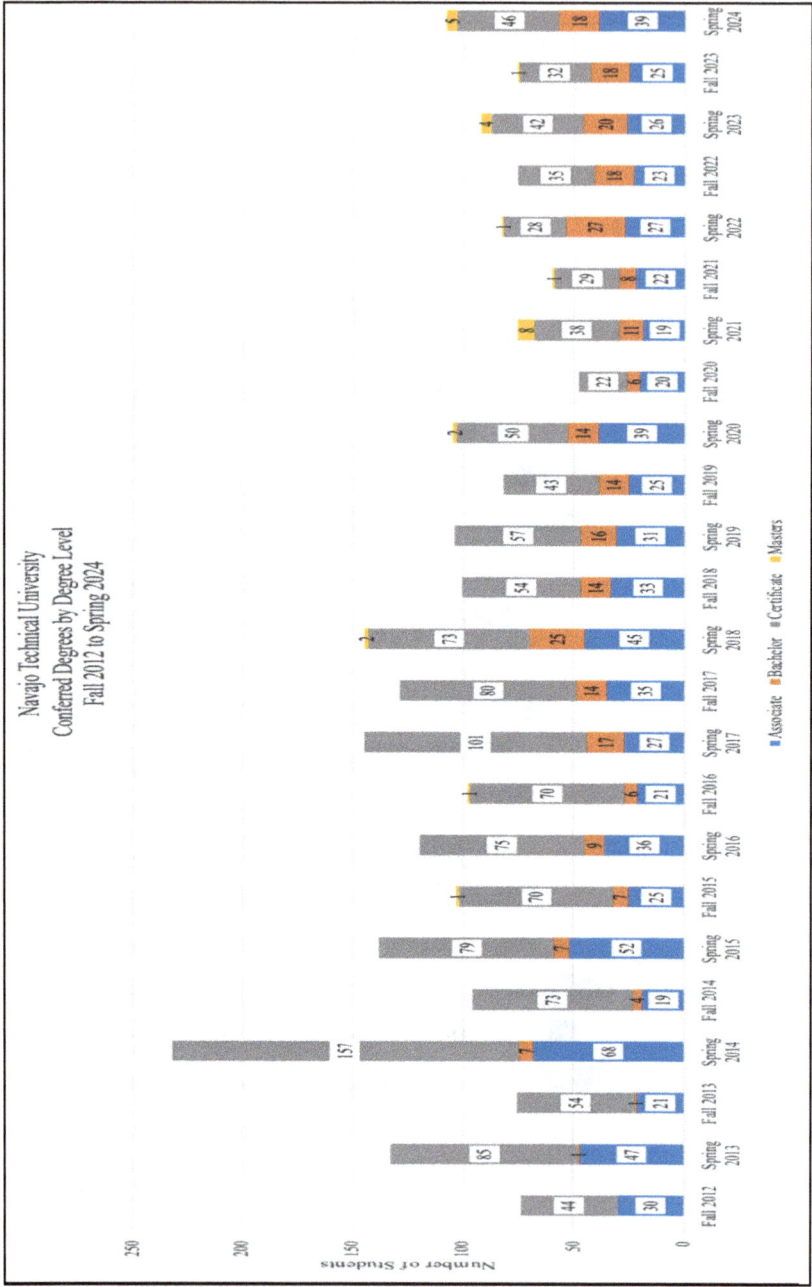

Navajo Technical University
Conferred Degrees by Degree Level
Fall 2012 to Spring 2024

Fall to Spring Persistence of First Time In College, Full-Time, and Degree Seeking Students

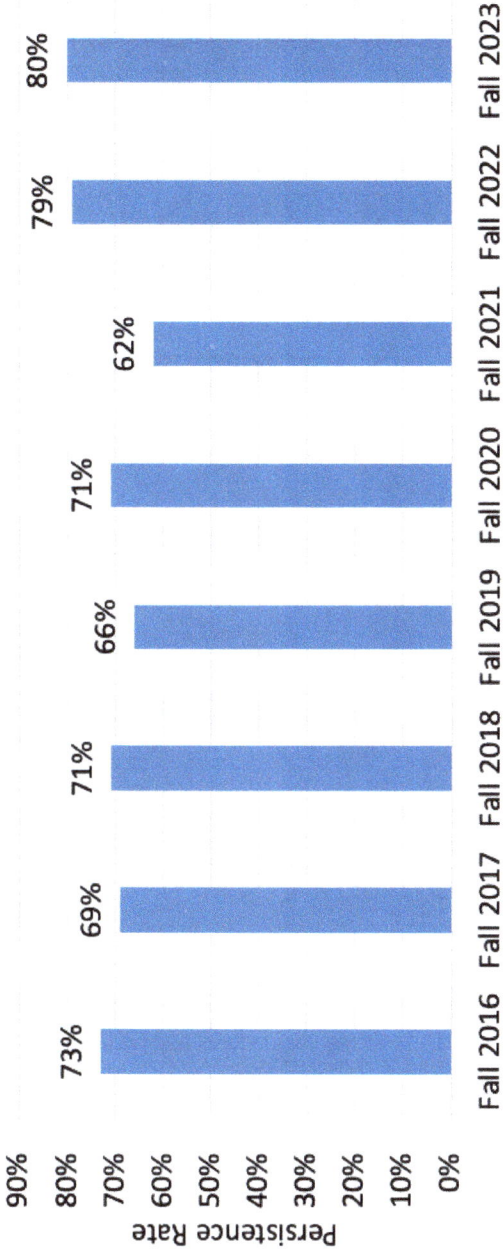

	Fall 2016	Fall 2017	Fall 2018	Fall 2019	Fall 2020	Fall 2021	Fall 2022	Fall 2023
Persistence Rate	73%	69%	71%	66%	71%	62%	79%	80%

Fall to Fall Retention of First Time In College, Full-Time, and Degree Seeking Students

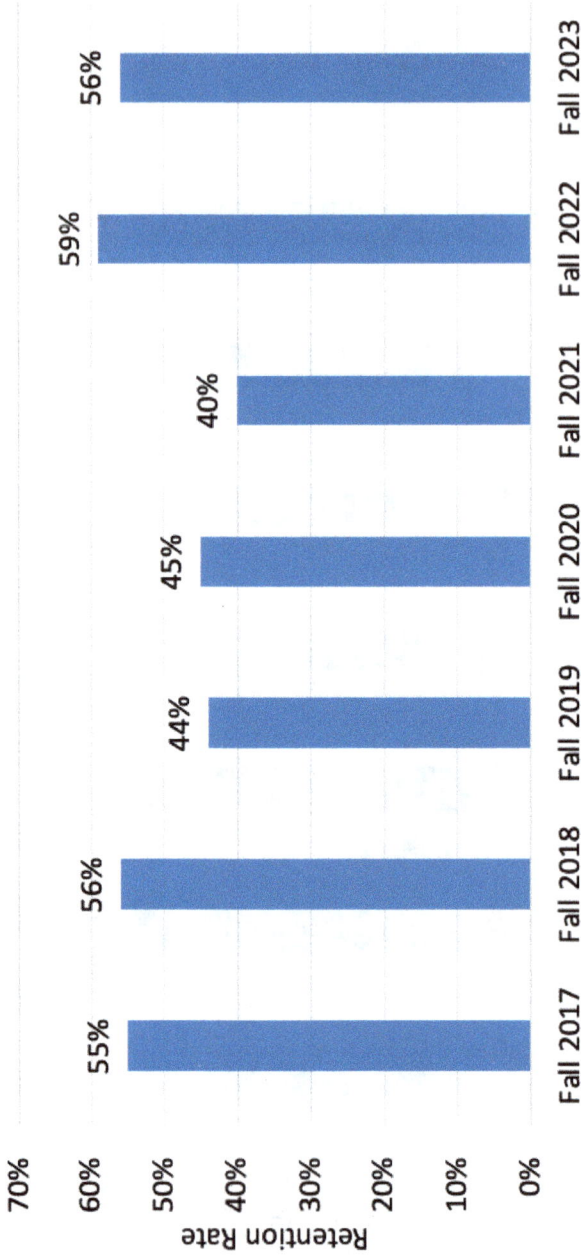

Term	Retention Rate
Fall 2017	55%
Fall 2018	56%
Fall 2019	44%
Fall 2020	45%
Fall 2021	40%
Fall 2022	59%
Fall 2023	56%

If NTU is going to meet the goal of graduating an increasing number of Navajo students, the first essential step in that process is to increase persistence and retention rates. This has been an intensive effort at the university. Both in-year persistence and retention rates, from fall into spring, have been improving. As is true across all higher education, the pandemic severely hurt retention between fall and fall. The effort to improve those rates is still a work in progress, but significant progress has been made.

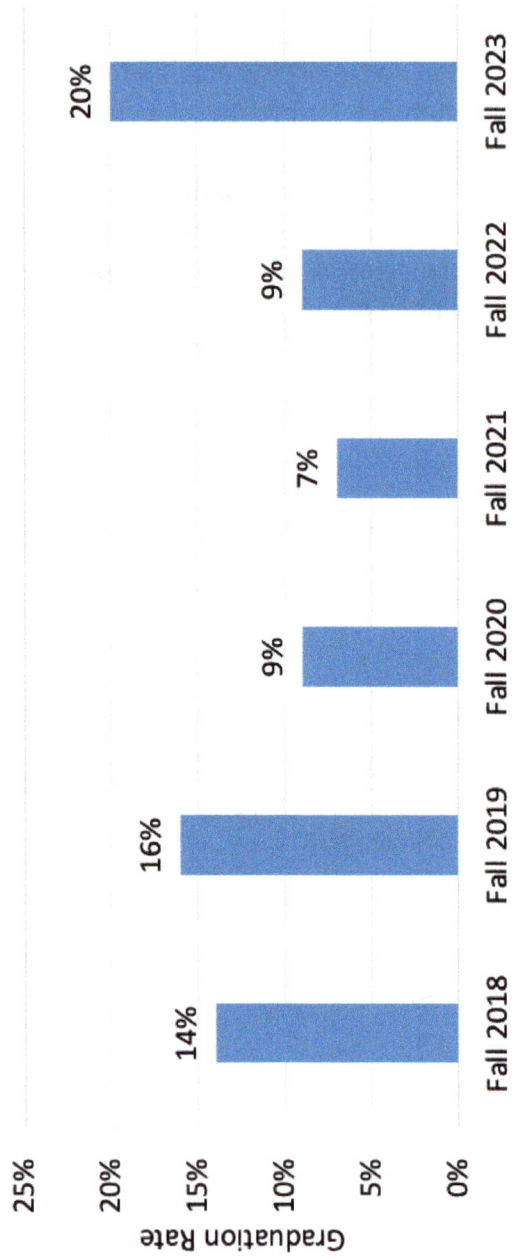

Navajo Technical University's Graduation Rate Trend (source: IPEDS)

Tribal college and university graduation rates have historically not matched those of most mainstream universities. There are several factors that have led to this challenge, which are not unique to TCUs. TCU rates are not unusual when rates for students from poverty-level and minority communities are analyzed separately from overall rates in mainstream colleges and universities. At NTU, Student Services has been working extremely hard to improve graduation rates, and significant results from that work are beginning to be visible.

Top Ten Majors at NTU 2024

NTU's Top Ten Majors	#
Early Childhood Multicultural Education	140
Business Administration	93
Welding	84
Nursing Assistant	65
Administrative Office Specialist	59
General Studies	58
Electrical Trades	46
Culinary Arts	44
Accounting	44
Automotive Technology	38

First Time in College Students, Top Ten Majors	#
Welding	29
Electrical Trades	21
Nursing Assistant	20
Automotive Technology	14
General Studies	13
Registered Nursing	8
Early Childhood Multicultural Education	8
Culinary Arts	7
Veterinary Technician	7
Construction Technology	6
Computer Science	5
Administrative Office Specialist	5

Continuing Students, Top Ten Majors	#
Early Childhood Multicultural Education	95
Business Administration	62
Administrative Office Specialist	41
Welding	39
Nursing Assistant	33
General Studies	32
Culinary Arts	28
Accounting	23
Biology	20
Information Technology Technician	17
Registered Nursing	17
Electrical Engineering	16

Transfer- In Students, Top Ten Majors	#
Early Childhood Multicultural Education	22
Business Administration	16
Accounting	15
Welding	10
Administrative Office Specialist	8
Registered Nursing	8
Counseling- substance use disorder	6
Electrical Trades	6
Nursing Assistant	6
General Studies	5
Culinary Arts	5
Counseling	4
Biology	4
Heavy Equipment Operator/ CDL	4
Law Advocate	4

Portraits of NTU Graduates

The most important task that NTU embraces is to ensure the university is providing a world-class education that allows its graduates to land good careers in their chosen fields. Choosing just a few of the thousands and thousands of graduates from the university to feature in a book like this is absurd in some ways. So many students have spent years earning their degree and then gone on to secure outstanding careers, leaving any of them out is unfortunate. However, if all graduates that deserve profiling were profiled, the book would never be published.

As the effort to assemble this book was undertaken, another challenge was to get a broad enough range of graduates from different degree programs to ensure the flavor of what our graduates are achieving is represented. Also important is to give an idea about how the university with its accomplishments is serving the Navajo Nation, regions surrounding the nation, and the United States. The following portraits are a representation and not a complete picture. The following graduates deserve to be honored, but the accomplishment Navajo Tech has achieved is larger than what is represented here.

Dwight Carlson

Environmental Science Major

Dwight Carlston is a member of the Navajo Nation, specifically from the To'aheedliinii (Water Flows Together) and Ts'ah yisk'idnii (Sage Brush Hill) clans. He comes from Falcon Nest near Twin Lakes, New Mexico. Dwight graduated from Tohatchi High School, where he excelled in Cross-Country.

After high school, Dwight attended Fort Lewis College in Durango, Colorado, where he was accepted to compete in Cross-Country. However, feeling out of place, he decided to work and save money for a different school. During this time, he enrolled in Navajo Technical College and took carpentry classes under the instruction of Tom Bebo.

Having been around livestock his entire life, Dwight eagerly joined the Rodeo Team at NTC. He began competing in bull riding across the southwestern United States. "At the time, it was a win-win situation, as I had the opportunity to engage in extracurricular activities like rodeo while continuing my studies," Mr. Carlston explained.

In 2009, Dwight earned his certificate in carpentry and subsequently transferred to Haskell Indian Nations University, where he enrolled in the environmental science program. During his first year, he was fortunate to win the men's cross-country conference championship. Feeling confident in his running abilities, Dwight returned home and re-enrolled at Navajo Technical University to continue pursuing his two-year environmental science program.

Dwight worked diligently to complete his associate degree in environmental science and pursue his bachelor's degree thereafter. Recognizing his outstanding achievements among all tribal colleges and universities,

AIHEC honored him as the Student of the Year during the 2010 AIHEC conference in Green Bay, Wisconsin. Consequently, Dwight was elected as the Student Congress President and the President of the NTU Student Senate, serving two terms in each role. "It was a lot to manage, representing many tribal colleges and universities while providing services and opportunities for students, both on and off the reservation," Dwight reflected.

In 2016, Dwight earned his baccalaureate degree in Environmental Science. He served as the Student Senate President during the campaign to change the institution's name before the Board of Regents and the Navajo Nation Council. During these sessions in Window Rock, AZ, NTU President Dr. Elmer Guy often invited Dwight to advocate on behalf of the university. "We successfully transitioned the name from Navajo Technical College to Navajo Technical University, and I am proud to have contributed to that change," Dwight stated.

After completing his studies at NTU, Dwight enrolled in a Master degree program in Environmental Science at the University of Georgia in Athens, GA, specializing in Agriculture Leadership, Environmental Education, and Communication.

Dwight is now a senior environmental inspector in the Arizona Department of Agriculture's air quality program, serving within the Gila River Indian Community. He also represents the National Tribal Air Association. "In this role, my focus is on protecting the environment and ensuring that companies and facilities do not pollute our water or air or contribute harmful pesticides," Dwight explains.

For the past four and a half years, Dwight has collaborated closely with the Environmental Protection Agency, industrial businesses, state regulatory agencies, and community stakeholders to ensure compliance with environmental standards across various sectors in Phoenix, AZ. Utilizing his expertise, he conducts thorough inspections, identifies areas of non-compliance, and develops corrective action plans to mitigate environmental risks.

"All I wanted to do was move forward in working with environmental issues and to ensure that the environment has a voice and an advocate. I always visit NTU whenever I get the chance. Recently, I had the opportunity to be a guest speaker during the fall commencement. It's rewarding to talk to students and share my experiences there. I show them that while NTU might not be a huge campus, it is close to home and truly is what you make of it," Dwight concludes.

Jared Ribble

Information Technology Major Master's Degree in Management Information Systems

Jared Ribble has been responsible for putting together one of the most advanced technology infrastructures at any university in the Southwest. NTU's Information Technology (IT) department envisions a future where vibrant learning communities have unrestricted access to personalized information, free from technological and geographical limitations.

Originally from Little Water, NM, Jared grew up near Crownpoint, NM. After graduating high school, he aspired to attend medical school at the University of New Mexico in Albuquerque. However, on his first day, he felt overwhelmed by the rigorous curriculum and the presence of so many students, leading to self-doubt and a sense of distance from home. To tackle these challenges, he enrolled at UNM-Gallup to complete his core medical classes.

During his studies, Jared discovered Crownpoint Institute of Technology (CIT) and decided to take several programming and computer courses relevant to his medical degree. While attending CIT, he developed a passion for technology and worked for the Navajo Nation workforce in the IT office. This experience sparked his interest in computers and fueled a desire to learn new skills during his free time.

Initially, Jared's mother was against his decision to attend the school; she believed that pursuing an education at CIT would not lead to anything positive. However, at 21, Jared was hired as an IT technician, where he shared his ideas for improving data transfer and expanding the university's broadband infrastructure to enhance Internet services.

Jared's mother eventually apologized, saying, "I want to apologize to you, son. I didn't believe you could achieve anything or succeed within that organization." Jared saw her apology as a humble beginning and recognized the growth of NTU and its potential. This acknowledgment helped him in his role as IT Director.

The IT department collaborates with nearly every aspect of the university—from accounting and operations to human resources and supply chain management—to develop the tools and processes needed for collecting, storing, managing, securing, and reporting vital information essential for running the organization. For Jared, this work is fulfilling. "Getting paid for your hobby makes it easy to do, and my kids see the work ethic," he explained.

As the IT Director, Jared aims to foster growth within the department. He observes his employees tackling daily cybersecurity initiatives and developing a database for missing Navajo children and women on campus. He has experienced growing pains navigating the challenges IT departments face. "Eventually, there will be days when the university will thrive, but in the IT world, things can take a year to reach that point. As technologies evolve, it doesn't happen overnight," Jared noted.

Jared intends to build his team at Chinle's instructional site, with one member overseeing the IT department at the sister site. He believes in "exploiting the norm and researching to fix the problems of running a business. Simply put, we must break things to fix the problems," Jared expressed.

With technology constantly evolving, Jared keeps his team informed about upcoming training sessions. He believes his department has the mechanical aptitude to learn and grow rather than going outside NTU and hiring outside contractors. "It's a talent for working with machines and on computers to understand how they function so that you troubleshoot technical issues and learn new technologies related to hardware and software," Jared explained.

Jared earned his bachelor's degree from Salish Kootenai College in Montana by taking online courses while fulfilling work responsibilities at the Crownpoint campus. Before returning to NTU from the Gallup campus, Jared had a dislike for writing and literature. However, he came to recognize the importance of these subjects in teaching his staff about human nature and effective communication, prompting him to take several classes at Western Governors University in Salt Lake City.

As an alumnus of NTU, he completed his master's degree in Management Information Systems and is now considering pursuing a Ph.D. in Technology at Purdue University. He said, "I need to finish some projects before I can devote my time to furthering my education." When asked if earning his master's degree changed him, Jared replied, "I am glad I earned the degree, but the next day, it was back to the usual routine. It's important because we are well-known in various parts of the country due to our research."

The next significant step for NTU's IT department is to implement network redundancy. Jared envisions establishing NTU's fiber network in major cities, ensuring operations retain capabilities to do its tasks despite failure. "More redundancy equals more reliability. It's a hobby!" Jared concluded.

Jacqueline Lee

Certified Nursing Assistant (CNA) Major

Jacqueline Lee hails from Three Turkey Ruins, Arizona, located approximately 20 miles southeast of Chinle, near a prominent mountain called Fluted Rock. The local population is about 30, all closely related through family ties. Jacqueline is a Todich'ii'nii (Bitter Water Clan) member and was born for the To Baazhni'azhi (Two Who Came to Water Clan). Her maternal grandparents belong to the Kinyaa'aanii (Towering House Clan), while her paternal grandparents are from the Todik'ozhi (Salt Water Clan).

Jacqueline sought a stable job in a healthcare facility to provide for her family after she finished school at the Chinle instructional site and has always wanted to help others. As a certified nursing assistant (CNA), she works under the direction of a nurse, providing patient care and comfort. Her responsibilities in the hospital include taking vital signs, transporting patients within the facility, and monitoring intake and output. She excels in building strong interpersonal relationships with patients. "NTU changed my life in many ways, providing personal and professional growth. It helped me with career preparation, self-awareness, and the discipline to work hard," Jacqueline shares.

At NTU, Jacqueline was goal-oriented and effectively managed her time between family and work. She believes that earning her CNA degree has impacted her life and benefited her community by allowing her to apply for jobs on the Navajo Reservation. "It also encourages employers to hire locals rather than seeking employees from far away," Jacqueline states.

"I owe my parents a debt of gratitude for encouraging me to return to college and giving me their constant prayers. I want to provide for my daughter, who significantly motivates my determination to succeed. My partner, Kyler, has also played an instrumental role in my education by providing transportation, financial support, and endless encouragement."

Jacqueline found the Chinle NTU instructional site very convenient and never felt overwhelmed by her assignments. "I had extra time to raise my daughter, study, and commute from my remote home to attend classes," she expresses.

She advises incoming students to always believe in themselves and maintain confidence. "When you feel lost, asking questions and seeking help is crucial. Stay strong-minded regardless of the circumstances and work hard for your future."

"I would like to thank everyone at the Chinle instructional site, especially the nursing staff. I appreciate the two RNs who worked 8–10-hour shifts and took extra time to educate us nursing students. I also want to thank the nursing advisor for ensuring each student had the necessary credentials and paperwork to complete the course. Lastly, I want to thank my colleagues in the CNA program; we started as strangers but finished the program as a family," Jacqueline expressed.

Jacqueline graduated from Chinle High School in 2014 and participated in a dual enrollment program with Northland Pioneer College. After working for two years as a retail manager, she pursued a more fulfilling career. She enrolled in the Certified Nursing Assistant (CNA) program at NTU in Chinle. She is proud to have graduated with a 3.8 GPA and made the Dean's List in Fall 2024. Jacqueline is currently majoring in nursing and is eager to obtain her Bachelor of Science in Nursing (BSN).

"Thanks to NTU, I have gained new perspectives on life and made significant progress in my field of study," she indicated in an interview.

Marcie Vandever

Dual Advanced Manufacturing Technology and Industrial Engineering Major

Marcie Vandever is dedicated to improving industrial production processes. She enhances efficiency, safety, and cost-effectiveness through thoughtful design and analysis. With her strong analytical skills and engineering background, she eagerly confronts complex manufacturing challenges, aiming to make a meaningful impact.

Originally from Smith Lake, NM, Marcie did not initially plan to become an industrial engineer. Instead, she considered it a strategic choice to create better opportunities after graduation. She began her studies in the Advanced Manufacturing Technology program at Navajo Technical University (NTU), where she learned about the importance of the Accreditation Board for Engineering and Technology (ABET) in facilitating pathways to four-year institutions.

At NTU, Marcie became a dual major and took on the role of Research Assistant, where she supports various research projects, machinery, and software. "Thanks to ABET accreditation, I became a dual major and started taking classes in the Industrial Engineering program. Earning an Industrial Engineering degree has opened many doors for me, particularly in the government sector," she explained.

In her role as a process engineer with the division of Honeywell that is a management and operations contractor with the federal government, Marcie applies her educational background to her job. "I can utilize what I've learned. My knowledge of manufacturing supports my fellow engineers," she remarked. Her dual degrees provide her with significant advantages, contributing to various aspects of her work in manufacturing and industry.

Earning her degree has also had a positive impact on Marcie's community. She dedicates her time to volunteering at St. Bonaventure in Thoreau, NM and local schools, where she serves as a judge for science fairs. Each year, along with a few team members, she volunteers for the regional science fair, and she recruits judges from her workplace to support the event. Additionally, as an avid runner, she coaches the cross-country program at St. Bonaventure, advocating for NTU, and encouraging many runners and students to consider attending the university.

At NTU, Marcie is furthering her education by working toward a certificate in the welding program. "I try to stay connected with the university. I continue to attend career fairs and engage with my colleagues and students. I remain proactive in my research and aim to make improvements in our Navajo communities," Marcie shared.

By introducing students to advanced manufacturing processes, such as 3D printing, Marcie hopes to inspire the younger generation to pursue careers in fields like metrology, robotics, and engineering. "I am open to the opportunity to teach. The youth today often don't realize potential career paths that are available until someone shows them," Vandever stated.

Marcie graduated from Thoreau High School in 2000 and participated in a dual enrollment program with Navajo Technical University. She works as a process engineer for Honeywell FM&T (Federal Manufacturing and Technology), a contractor for the Department of Energy's Kansas City National Security Campus. Marcie is one of six siblings and grew up in a family that raised livestock. She graduated from Navajo Technical University with both an associate and bachelor's degree.

"I enjoy my current role as an industrial engineering student. I find the processes very meticulous, and I take pride in being detail oriented. I am also proud to work in New Mexico and this industry," Marcie explained.

As the campus manager for NTU, Marcie advocates for the Kansas City National Security Campus. She recognizes the value student internships and entry-level employees bring to our diverse workforce, especially during local career fairs and site visits.

"Thanks to the Center for Advanced Manufacturing, we have access to world-class advanced manufacturing technology, which is essential for training the space industry workforce for tomorrow."

Hansen Tapaha

Electrical Engineering Major

Hansen Tapaha is a proud graduate of the Electrical Engineering program at NTU and a native of Balakai Point, AZ. He is a Tsi'naajinii (Black Streak Wood People) clan member, with the Ta'neeszahnii (Tangle People) as his maternal clan. His maternal grandparents are Tse'nijikini (Honey Combed Rock People), while his paternal grandparents belong to the Deeschnii'nii (Start at the Red Streak People) clan. Hansen is also an alumnus of Ganado High School.

After graduating from high school, Mr. Tapaha enrolled at the University of New Mexico (UNM-Gallup) branch to pursue a career in construction. He worked at local fast-food restaurants to help pay for his tuition. He faced several challenges during his studies but ultimately earned an associate degree in General Studies. He takes pride in being the first-generation college graduate in his family.

After graduating from UNM, Tapaha applied his knowledge as an electrical technician in various jobs. Many of his colleagues helped him troubleshoot, diagnose, and install wiring. However, he faced a health setback and was hospitalized for about a month.

During his recovery, Tapaha married his long-time girlfriend. They agreed it would benefit him to further his education and explore a different career path. He enrolled at Navajo Technical University (NTU) to obtain his Commercial Driver's License (CDL) and a degree in heavy equipment operation. Unfortunately, the university did not allow him to enroll due to COVID-19 restrictions and his status as an out-of-state student.

In the spring of 2015, the program advisor at Navajo Technical University (NTU) discussed academic goals with Tapaha and recommended that he connect with Dr. Peter Romine, who had recently launched the Electrical Engineering program. Tapaha became one of Dr. Romine's first students in this new program. "The program had just started, so I dedicated myself to learning as much as possible about hardware and software. We didn't have access to these resources on the reservation, and books were my primary source of information," Tapaha explained.

While attending NTU, Tapaha collaborated with various departments and worked on numerous projects, mainly through the fabrication laboratory alongside Scott Halliday, the Director of the Advanced Manufacturing Center. Mr. Tapaha and his fellow students participated in the Maker Faire in Washington, D.C. This event brings together technology enthusiasts, crafters, educators, tinkerers, hobbyists, engineers, science clubs, authors, artists, students, and commercial exhibitors. At the Maker Faire, Tapaha and his colleagues showcased projects involving laser scanning, 3D modeling, and 3D printing.

"Overall, the Maker Faire was a fantastic experience for all the students. We had the opportunity to present our work, gain new knowledge, and, most importantly, meet Director John P. Holdren, who served as the Assistant to the President for Science and Technology and was the Director of the White House Office of Science and Technology Policy during the Obama administration," Tapaha said.

In the fall of 2017, Hansen graduated from NTU with his friends and was among the first recipients of a bachelor's degree in electrical engineering. Before graduating, Mr. Tapaha completed several internships at the Johnson Space Center in Houston, TX and at the Army Research Laboratory in Huntsville, AL where he primarily focused on programming and running simulators for military technology.

During his time in Huntsville, Hansen felt a strong bond with his colleagues and decided to inquire about job openings. "I wanted to ask for a position because I felt like family working there. I appreciated how I was treated and how others were treated," Tapaha explained.

On February 5, 2018, Hansen began his civil service and accepted a job offer at the Army Research Laboratory in Huntsville, AL. He develops software with facial recognition capabilities in this role and works as a hardware integration engineer. Later, his wife and children joined him. "Overall, I work as a team member; in this sense, I contribute to bringing American soldiers back home safely. It makes me a proud citizen to see what I have accomplished in technology toward that goal," Hansen concluded.

Twila Largo

Administrative Office Technology Major

Twila Largo is Kiyaani and Ashiihi. Her maternal grandparents are Kinlacheeni, and her paternal grandparents are Tachninii. She resides in Crownpoint, NM. She is originally from Ahwatukee, AZ, where she got her education while growing up in the Kyrene School District in West Chandler, AZ. Twila graduated from Mountain Pointe High School, home of the Pride.

During her education at Mountain Pointe, Twila grew up with her siblings in a diverse environment rich in culture, history, and sports. This experience highlighted the challenges of being responsible.

In 2013, Twila moved back to Crownpoint to live with her sister because she missed the Navajo culture. With the support of her family and parents, she enrolled at Navajo Technical University to pursue her studies in early childhood education. However, wanting to help others, Twila quickly transferred to the School of Business.

While at the university, Twila interned as an administrative assistant under George LaFrance, the Athletics Director. She gained valuable experience during this internship, stating, "He taught me how to manage events, understand the attendees, and guide them around campus." Since then, Twila has embraced a healthy lifestyle and encourages other students to do the same by participating in sports and workouts.

In addition to her internship, she was an active secretary in the Student Senate, where she took detailed notes on key points, decisions, action items, and essential discussions during meetings. Twila ensured a record was kept of what was discussed and identified and who was responsible for each task, effectively capturing critical information, including student concerns. Twila remarked, "The difficult part was balancing work, parenting, and being a student. Being part of the team and receiving that recognition was good enough for me."

Twila pursued her education and resources, focusing on developing the ethics, character, and integrity needed to make a meaningful difference. In addition, she gained valuable experience working as an Administrative Assistant under Virginia Edgewater in Student Services, assisting with events across various departments on campus.

During the COVID-19 pandemic in 2020, Twila balanced raising her children with caring for livestock. She earned her associate degree in Administrative Office Technology, which equipped her with valuable skills relevant to today's workplace. After graduating, she joined her mother at Victoria's Pizza, where they collaborated to create a business plan that initially started as a food truck and eventually evolved into a revenue generating business in Crownpoint.

Using her degree, Twila applied to the university and worked under Dr. Wesley Thomas while commuting from Arizona. She played a crucial role in establishing the NTU Hogan by managing funds and coordinating tasks for events held inside the Hogan. This included organizing food, tracking expenses, and even purchasing a buffalo hide, which is still used in today's graduation ceremony.

As the Administrative Assistant for the Vice President of Operations, Twila views her current role as a steppingstone toward various careers in education, including education administration, school counseling, and social work. She continues to help others by managing budgets, schedules, disciplinary actions, and event planning. "Keen attention to detail, excellent organizational skills and a passion for connecting with students and teachers are essential qualities for an administrative assistant," Twila concluded.

Warlance Chee

Master of Arts in Diné Culture, Language, and Leadership

Warlance Chee aims to provide traditional teachings and services to the urban Diné communities within and around Albuquerque, New Mexico.

Chee currently serves as the project lead for *Saad K'idlyé*, a grassroots organization dedicated to creating and establishing a Diné language nest in Albuquerque, New Mexico, where his wife and four children reside. *Saad K'idlyé*'s language nest opened its doors on August 15, 2022, and has experienced a steady increase in attendance, including families who are expecting a baby, as well as newborns and toddlers. "Children at the nest are spoken to in their traditional language throughout the day and are taught basic commands and responses," Warlance explained.

"With all my experience in the education system, including the Bureau of Indian Education (BIA) and charter schools, I can see little equity for our language. Most language classes last only thirty minutes per week," Chee stated.

"We want our kids to learn the Diné language. Some individuals are satisfied with learning the basic vocabulary for colors, shapes, and sizes—just the bare minimum in language education. The children spend almost half the day at the nest, and none of the parents speak Navajo," Chee remarked. Warlance added, "That's where the hard work begins—with the parents."

As *Saad K'idlyé* enters its third year, the Diné language nest has improved its effort to engage families by encouraging attendance and participation. Warlance aims to ensure that parents are committed and fulfilling their responsibilities. "We are here to produce first-language speakers and to encourage the continued use of the language at home," Warlance stated.

Enrolling in the program entails many commitments and expectations. Various events, classes, projects, and other programming are planned. Babies and infants absorb language easily by being surrounded by it and spoken to regularly.

Warlance is from Lake Valley, New Mexico, and is a member of the Tsénahabiłnii and born for the Kinłichíi'nii clan. He graduated from Lake Valley Navajo School and then attended Navajo Preparatory School in Farmington, New Mexico. After high school, Warlance enrolled at the University of New Mexico, earning a Bachelor of Arts degree in American Studies with a minor in Native American Studies. He then obtained a Master of Arts in Diné Culture, Language, and Leadership from NTU.

Warlance has worked as a Diné language and culture teacher for nine years. He has taught at various institutions, including Cuba Independent Schools, Tóhajiilee Community School, and most recently, at the Native American Community Academy (NACA) in Albuquerque, New Mexico. Currently, he is participating in a two-year fellowship with the NACA Inspired Schools Network (NISN).

"I hope the community back home, or around the Navajo Nation, is looking to do something similar to our language nest," Chee emphasized.

Terri Ami

Culinary Arts and Baking Dual Majors

Terri Ami is a member of the Ashihii (Salt People) and was born into the Shash Dine'e (Bear People) clan. She resides in Albuquerque, NM, but originally hails from Crownpoint. Terri received her education at various high schools in the area and eventually earned her GED in Window Rock, AZ.

After completing high school, Terri decided to further her studies in Scottsdale, AZ, motivated by her passion for early childhood education. To support her educational goals as a college student, she worked as a barista in the Scottsdale area and was employed at several coffee shops.

After spending many years in Phoenix, Terri began to feel insecure and yearned for her family. This prompted her to return home, especially as she was dealing with the slow decline of her grandfather's health. Terri cherished her time at home, where she cared for her grandfather, honoring and valuing him daily.

After her grandfather's passing, Terri felt lost for a considerable amount of time. She pursued an automotive technician certificate at Navajo Technical University to find direction. However, securing a job proved challenging due to the increased competition and growth in the automotive industry. This led Terri to explore another passion: Culinary Arts, which allowed her to enhance her cooking skills. "I wanted to continue my education and go as far as I could, taking as many classes as I wanted, with the support of my colleagues and Chef Bob," Terri explained.

At the start of her culinary journey, Terri encountered numerous challenges in the kitchen. "Everyone has their way of learning, and personalities tend to change in the kitchen. It's a learning process about food and people," she stated.

Terri completed her dual Culinary Arts and Baking degree at NTU. During her studies, she gained valuable experience with SkillsUSA, where she honed her skills in fine dining and achieved second place for two consecutive years. Additionally, she actively participated in the annual Chocolate Fantasy, sponsored by the New Mexico Museum of Natural History Foundation, serving as a student baker for three consecutive years.

After graduating, Terri held various kitchen positions, including an Executive Chef role at Diné College. Although she had little experience at the time, she successfully managed all aspects of the kitchen independently, which provided a significant learning opportunity during her year there. NMS Food Services, which provides food services to local schools and businesses, recognized Terri's work at NTU and offered her a job in Anchorage, Alaska.

Using her degree, Terri worked in several schools across Alaska, preparing meals for students from dawn until dusk. She spent time in towns like Bethel and Nome, where she was assigned to stay during the COVID-19 pandemic. Terri faced several challenges during her isolation, including limited communication due to a lack of Internet access and transportation. She worked alone for the Nome school district, covering both the grade school and high school kitchens while managing the logistics of driving between different sites.

With only two co-workers to assist her, Terri became physically, mentally, and emotionally burnt out during the pandemic. "I just needed to slow down. I wanted to go home after the pandemic restrictions lifted, so I took it when I saw my opportunity. I went home," Terri stated.

After being home for a few months, Terri revisited NTU to reconnect with friends and colleagues. Eventually, Chef Robert Witte, Master Technical Instructor, suggested she contact Sysco, a leading food service distributor. Although initially hesitant, she became a Sales Consultant, responsible for promoting the company's products and services and building relationships with new and existing accounts. Terri continues to advance her career by managing deliveries and driving profitable sales growth around the Navajo Nation, ensuring that everyone gets fed.

"Through everything, good or bad, the experiences I went through all happened for a reason. Sometimes, we make mistakes and must take a step back to observe those errors. I've learned valuable lessons in various situations, especially when placed in a role I know nothing about. You have to figure it out. In life, you learn things on your own," Terri concluded.

Wayant Billey

Chemistry Major

Wayant Billey's academic journey began in Automotive Technology at NTU, driven by an early interest in energy systems and mechanical applications. However, his career trajectory was profoundly altered after encountering the innovative research emerging from the NEST Lab— particularly the synthesis and electrochemical characterization of biofuels, a research theme closely tied to the needs of both sustainable energy development and tribal economic resilience. Inspired by this work, Wayant made the academic leap from Automotive Technology (an associate degree program) into NTU's Bachelor of Science Chemistry program.

Once integrated into the NEST Lab, Wayant underwent a rigorous, hands-on training regimen to build both technical competency and research independence. His training covered electrochemical techniques, material characterization, fuel cell testing, and the synthesis and analysis of biofuels derived from locally available biomass resources. This interdisciplinary exposure broadened Wayant's scientific understanding and connected his research work directly to his Navajo community's energy needs, fostering a scientific purpose rooted in environmental sustainability.

Wayant's research outputs quickly garnered national recognition. He became a frequent presenter at the annual conferences of AIHEC, where his research presentations on electrochemical sensors research earned top honors in the Undergraduate Research Competitions (2024).

Throughout his undergraduate studies, Wayant's research progression was both vertically integrated (building deep expertise within electrochemical biofuels research) and horizontally expansive (exploring interdisciplinary applications across environmental science, energy systems, and materials chemistry). The mentoring from Dr. Thiagarajan Soundappan he received also equipped him with the scholarly tools to author research abstracts, co-develop technical reports, and effectively communicate his research findings to scientific and community audiences.

Wayant's story is not only one of individual academic transformation from a trade major but also represents a foundational milestone in NTU's Chemistry program. It demonstrates how research mentorship at a tribal university can catalyze academic mobility and expand the horizons of STEM education for Native American students. Through his work at the NEST Lab, Wayant transformed from an Automotive Technology student interested in biofuels to a nationally recognized undergraduate researcher and a trailblazer for NTU chemistry students.

Wayant is currently preparing to pursue doctoral studies. Wayant has two peer-reviewed research publications in the prestigious ECS Sensors Plus journal (part of the Electrochemical Society, USA). His long-term academic goal is to join the PhD program at Harvard University's School of Engineering and Applied Sciences. This ambition, built upon years of intensive mentorship, nationally recognized research achievements, and a deep commitment to using science for community benefit, places Wayant at the forefront of NTU's emerging generation of STEM leaders.

Daylana Hanna

Environmental Science and Natural Resources Major

Dalyna Hannah is from Ramah, NM. She is Naakai dine'e (Mexican People Clan) and is born for Dibe lizhini (Black Sheep Clan). Her maternal grandparents belong to the Kinyaa'aanii (Towering House) clan, while her paternal grandparents are from the Tsi'naajinii (Black Streak Wood People) clan.

Dalyna graduated from Ramah High School in 2015, the home of the Mustangs. After high school, she earned an Associate of Applied Science and a bachelor's degree in environmental science and Natural Resources from Navajo Technical University.

In addition to her academic success, Dalyna significantly contributed to several AIHEC volleyball and hand game championships while at NTU, and she placed third in the Research Competition at the Crownpoint Campus.

Dalyna has been accepted into the Bridge to Doctorate Program for her PhD in Natural Resources at the University of Idaho, where she has received a full tuition waiver and a stipend to support her studies. As a PhD student, she works on two chapters for a book being written in the Forestry department. The first chapter, "Determining the Effects of Mastication on Seedling Growth and Survival," focuses on the impact of growth in forests. Mastication refers to the mechanical breakdown of plant material. The second chapter, "Evaluating Technology by Using Smartphones' IMEI Sensors to Detect Seed Growth," explores innovative methods of measuring growth. Dalyna plans to extend her research to include a study on forestry within the Navajo Nation.

Additionally, Dalyna has been accepted as a tribal fellow in the College of Natural Resources at the University of Idaho, where she serves as an instructor involved in various projects and workshops.

She worked with the National Interagency Fire Center (NIFC) in Boise, ID, during the summer. The NIFC's fire management program aims to achieve practical fire suppression goals while efficiently and cost-effectively fulfilling a broad range of natural resource objectives. Dalyna hopes to secure a position with the NIFC after completing her education.

Dalyna has had numerous opportunities to gain extensive experience in environmental science. Along with her instructors, Dr. RoyChowdhury and Dr. Chischilly, she expresses gratitude for her experiences and encourages other students to pursue similar opportunities.

Robinson Tom

Biology Major

Robinson Tom is the first Biology major student recruited and formally trained in electrochemistry research at NTU's Nanoscale Electrochemical Science and Technology (NEST) Laboratory. As a student with limited prior exposure to electrochemical systems, Robinson's entry into the field represented a transformative opportunity for student development within a minority-serving institution.

Robinson trained at NTU in advanced electrochemical sensor development, lithium-ion batteries, electro-analytical techniques, and materials characterization. His training extended beyond the confines of the university laboratory through collaborative summer research placements at the U.S. Army Research Laboratory, where he gained exposure to large-scale, mission-driven electrochemistry research on aqueous lithium-ion batteries for U.S. Soldiers.

The culmination of this intensive mentorship was Robinson's first peer-reviewed publication in the internationally recognized *Journal of Power Sources*, a prestigious venue for applied electrochemical research. Robinson served as a co-author on this landmark publication alongside Dr. Thiagarajan Soundappan.

After graduating from NTU, Robinson was admitted as a post-baccalaureate research scholar at Harvard University in 2021. Throughout this period, Robinson continued to refine his research acumen, building upon the scientific foundation established at NTU while embracing new interdisciplinary challenges at Harvard.

This trajectory of scholarly development culminated in Robinson Tom's historic admission to the PhD program at the Harvard John A. Paulson School of Engineering and Applied Sciences in 2022, where he became the first graduate student from NTU to achieve such a distinction

Robinson's academic journey is further underscored by his service as a U.S. Army veteran. His army experience enriched his academic perspective by giving him leadership skills, resilience, and a strong sense of purpose. His dual identity as a veteran scholar and first-generation researcher amplifies his role as an ambassador of NTU's research excellence and as an inspirational case study for future students at the interface of STEM education, research, and public service.

Sheena Begay

Law Advocate Major Master's degree in Management Information Systems

Sheena Begay is Tl'aashchi'i (Red Cheek People) and is born for the Honaghaahnii (One-Who-Walks-Around). Her maternal grandfather is from the Dzihgha'i- Deeshchii'nii (White Mountain Apache adopted by the Start of the Red Streak People), and her paternal grandfather is Tachii'nii (Red Running into the Water People).

In the spring of 2006, Sheena Begay began her journey at CIT in Crownpoint during a transformative time for the institution.

She pursued a major in Law Advocate and earned an associate degree. Sheena comes from a rural area of the Navajo Nation, located between Rough Rock and Chilchinbeto, Arizona, and was already familiar with remote living. Raised in a household without indoor plumbing or electricity, her family—which included her parents and nine siblings—relied on hauling water for their daily needs and livestock. The nearest town with essential services was an hour away, which gave her a newfound appreciation for the conveniences available in her CIT dorm room, where even a tiny refrigerator brought her joy.

Her educational journey began after graduating from Monument Valley High School, Kayenta, Arizona. Sheena then attended the College of Eastern Utah in Blanding but was not prepared to live in a large city far from home. Ultimately, she returned to the College of Eastern Utah in the spring of 2006, intending to transfer to the University of Arizona but then heard about programs at CIT. Since it was a tribal college, that sounded like a place that might be more comfortable to attend. At that time, the institution lacked a Wellness Center, Library, or IT building, with the cafeteria as the primary event space.

"Drawing on my experiences from previous institutions, I actively worked to create student clubs and activities once I got to CIT and advocated for a dedicated Student Activities position, which I eventually secured," Sheena explained. Her involvement with the Student Senate led to significant achievements, including selecting the current NTU logo and participating in the institution's name change from CIT to Navajo Technical College.

As the Student Senate President, Sheena was pivotal in securing additional funding for student clubs, advocating for diverse meal plan options for dormitory residents, and spearheading the initiative to select a school mascot through student surveys. Her efforts culminated in the selection of the Skyhawks as the official mascot.

Sheena stated, "My commitment to enhancing student experiences originated from an important conversation with Tom Davis. During this discussion, I asked about student retention efforts at CIT. This inquiry laid the groundwork for my career and fostered a lifelong interest in understanding and improving student retention."

During Navajo Technical University's transition from a college to a university, Sheena encouraged her family and friends to explore the expanding program offerings. Her efforts resulted in recruiting fifteen close family members to NTU, fourteen of whom have either graduated or are on track to graduate.

Recognizing the need for higher qualifications as NTU's programs expanded, Sheena then pursued further education. She recounted, "While assisting my (future) spouse in crafting a compelling speech for his Student of the Year Award, in which he challenged the President of Navajo Technical College to offer bachelor's degrees in IT fields, my passion for social research led me to pursue a bachelor's degree at the University of New Mexico (UNM) in Albuquerque, NM."

Graduating from UNM in 2013, Sheena embraced motherhood, married her supportive husband, and continued to contribute to NTU's growth and success. In the fall of 2024, she received her master's degree in Management Information Systems from NTU with a 4.0 GPA in the program.

Today she is the Director of Institutional Data and Reporting at NTU. When asked about the evolving landscape of institutional data and the improvements she has implemented, Sheena emphasized the increasing importance of data-driven decision-making across all university levels. She stated, "Data has become an indispensable tool for shaping strategic initiatives and enhancing overall outcomes. The demand for data has significantly increased among faculty and staff and the Board of Regents, students, and other stakeholders."

Sheena welcomes and encourages data requests and conversations, as she firmly believes that data can drive positive change. She explained, "There is no way to act on an important issue if the problem is not identified. Once identified, the work begins.

"Furthermore, it's not always about addressing issues—it can also be about recognizing positive outcomes and finding ways to replicate them in other areas.

"One significant instance where data played a crucial role was our analysis of persistence, retention, and graduation rates at NTU several years ago. We aimed to identify the factors affecting students' ability to complete their degrees on time and to implement strategies to improve these rates," Sheena explained.

NTU uses Jenzabar as its Student Information System. Sheena utilizes Jenzabar's reporting tools, including student reports and Infomaker, to extract the necessary data. Once extracted, this data is transferred to Excel sheets, where she organizes and manages it for further analysis. She creates customized department data sheets using Pivot Tables. This powerful feature allows for extensive data analysis, enabling the identification of trends to generate insights and meet the specific needs of stakeholders.

From humble beginnings, running barefoot between red and white-streaked mesas, to serving as a director and member of the university President's cabinet, Sheena states, "I am profoundly grateful. I truly understand the meaning of 'Those who carry their water value every drop.' My parents, who earned their associate degrees while working full-time and driving long distances for night classes, remain a source of inspiration. Their unwavering encouragement and traditional Navajo teachings drive me to persevere, reminding me to seize every opportunity and never doubt my potential."

• C H A P T E R 8 •

Leadership at NTU

Provost, Dr. Colleen W. Bowman

Dr. Colleen Wilma Bowman is Naasht'ézhí Dowa:kwe (Zuni Corn Clan); Born for the Táchii'nii (Red Running into the Water People). Her maternal grandfathers are Ta'neeszahnii (Tangle, Badlands People) and her paternal grandfathers are Bit'ahnii (Folded Arms/Within His Cover People). Dr. Bowman was born in Utah and raised in the Navajo communities of Tuba City, Arizona, Shiprock, and Tohatchi, New Mexico.

She graduated salutatorian from the Navajo Methodist Mission School in Farmington, New Mexico and entered college at Eastern Montana College, now Montana State University in Billings, pursuing a degree in Elementary Education. She studied social justice at the American University in Washington, DC and the University of the Pacific-Stockton, California as a Hispanic, Asian, Native American (HANA) scholar. Beyond an associate degree in Secretarial Administration, she completed a bachelor degree in Business Administration with an emphasis in Human Resources Management. She returned to the Navajo Nation to serve youth and communities in the Shiprock Agency. Following her service to the Navajo

Nation, she continued her pursuit of higher learning at New Mexico State University and completed a master degree in Educational Management & Development and a doctorate degree in Educational Leadership and Administration. Her dissertation is titled, *"Defining Student Success through Navajo Perspectives"*.

Dr. Bowman credits her academic credentials to the support and encouragement of her family. According to Dr. Bowman, "A strong family foundation, grounded in faith and the love of learning, contributed to my academic achievements."

Since the Fall of 2019, Provost Bowman has actively maintained oversight of the Provost Leadership Team comprised of academic deans for undergraduate studies & graduate studies, dean of student services, manager of sponsored programs, and director of institutional data and reporting. Her involvement includes committee work, faculty and student matters, serving as principal investigator on tribal, state and federal grants to create highly qualified teachers, transform the tribal workforce, and participate on a global hydrogen development advisory council. She continues to expand her professional knowledge in online learning and developing effective modules and micro-lectures.

"Diverse involvement at the local, tribal, state, federal and global levels have provided me the platform to showcase NTU and its commitment to students, allowing them to grow, learn and contribute to society."

Dr. Bowman made history as the first female Native American Superintendent of the Central Consolidated School District. "It was an honor and privilege to serve preK-12 students and their communities. Through that experience, I am able to share possible ways NTU can create a pathway into higher education," she stated.

Utilizing all her various experiences, Dr. Bowman engages daily in meaningful conversations with students, staff, faculty, administrators, community members, and educational partners regarding continuous improvements for the university. "Navajo Technical University offers a rich learning experience to students while honoring their indigenous ways of knowing," Dr. Bowman concluded.

Vice President of Operations, Jason Arviso

Jason Arviso's father, Leonard D. Arviso, donated the land for Crownpoint Airport that allowed Navajo Skills Center to be located where Navajo Technical University still has its main campus. Working for the Navajo Nation, he was also instrumental in getting the skills center on the road toward becoming a university. Dr. Jason Arviso has therefore been associated in one way or another with NTU his entire life. He also comes by his role in education naturally enough since his mother was an educator when it was unusual for Navajo women to become either teachers or administrators.

Dr. Arviso grew up in Window Rock, Arizona where he graduated from Window Rock High School. After high school he enrolled in Ohio Dominican University in Columbus, Ohio and graduated with a baccalaureate degree in Management Information Systems. In Ohio, he became a System Administrator at Lucent Technologies and later took on the role of Software Verification Tester, working on network-driven applications designed by Lucent and Bell Labs Innovation Network Fault Management group.

When he returned to the Navajo Nation with his wife, Dr. Colleen Craig Arviso, the current Director of E-Learning at NTU, he was named the Director of Information Technology. When his title was changed to Director of Information Technology/Chief Technology Officer, he completed his Master of Science degree in Management Information at Capella University.

During his years working in IT for the Crownpoint Institute of Technology, then Navajo Technical College, and then NTU, he helped the school move from the era of modem-based Internet connectivity and unlicensed software usage to one of the most sophisticated technology infrastructures available to any U.S. institution of higher learning. He also helped develop and write several federally funded projects and served as the Prime Investigator (PI) for National Science Foundation (NSF) and other federal agency grants, handling all aspects of grant management.

He earned his EdD in 2023 in Leadership for Change from Fielding University after becoming NTU's Vice President of Operations. In his Vice-Presidential role, he is responsible for managing all operational units at the university, including the Finance Office, Human Resources, Information Technology, Marketing and Communications, Support Services, the Innovation Center, Auxiliary Services, and Sponsored Programs. He also works on economic development projects designed to increase the number of businesses and high skill/high wage jobs available for the Navajo people.

"As Navajo people we have a special opportunity," Jason said in an interview. "Navajo Tech is at the forefront of making that opportunity be more than sitting around in a committee room talking about it. We get things done here. We put one of the most advanced wireless networks available in the world at the time together and made it work and called it Internet to the Hogan. Our students are either earning a doctorate at the university or going on to earn advanced degrees at some of the most prestigious universities in the world like Harvard. We have labs in both Crownpoint and Chinle that are as advanced as any labs at any universities in the southwest. We have made project after project happen. Navajo Tech does. It doesn't just talk. The Navajo can own the future. We just need to make that happen."

He has made major presentations at different national forums over the years, including at the Super Computing Conference held in Seattle, Washington, the TeraGrid Conference held in 2007, and the Educause Conference in 2010, among others. He has also participated with efforts being made by the Navajo Nation to improve its Internet connectivity and increase cybersecurity and data sovereignty by serving on several committees.

CHAPTER 9

Prospectus for the Long and Short-term Development of Iíná, the Holding Company

Iíná was formed by the Board of Regents as a Limited Liability Company (LLC) that will compete in the private sector. It will have divisions formed because of opportunities created by the research and intellectual property flowing out of NTU. The holding company will create different divisions, to be called enterprises, based upon the market segments that different developments address. These enterprises will usually be characterized with a marketing name designed to appeal to that market segment. Iíná will also create products separate from the university if that will strengthen its competitive position in any market.

To launch Iíná, those charged with the task of bringing the holding company to life have created the first "enterprise," Navajo Advanced Manufacturing Enterprises (NAME), that will bring products to market. What follows is, first, the long-range plan for NAME that includes various sets of intellectual property and manufacturing capabilities created through the work of the Center of Advanced Manufacturing, directed by Harold "Scott" Halliday, at NTU. The first product line that will be sold by NAME is small batched custom powder for Metal AM machines that can produce parts for the aerospace, defense, higher education, and national laboratory industries.

Over the years of its operation, the Center for Advanced Manufacturing has become one of the most advanced labs of its type in the world. The expectation is that the marketing of products made possible by the highly skilled students that have earned degrees through work with that lab will help make the Navajo Nation and New Mexico, Arizona, and Utah where the Nation is located become an important Advanced Manufacturing Center in the United States.

Prospectus for Navajo Advanced Manufacturing Enterprises

Goal: Establish a leading-edge manufacturing business based upon Navajo Technical University's advanced manufacturing research and development to capture a significant research and development and product production presence in the overall advanced marketing marketplace emerging worldwide.

Navajo Advanced Manufacturing Enterprises (NAME) Abstract

Navajo Advanced Manufacturing will be organized to produce a broad range of advanced manufacturing services and products based upon the decades of research originally developed at the Advanced Manufacturing and Metrology laboratories at Navajo Technical University. This will be a separate business from the university designed to compete in the open marketplace for the services and products NAME will be designed to market.

Eventual Divisions within NAME will include the following:

A. Metal AM Powder Manufacturing
- Production. Initiating low production levels of metal AM powder with the potential for expansion.
- Preferred Vendor. Serving as a preferred vendor for Los Alamos National Laboratory (LANL) and academic institutions.

B. Space and Aerospace Company Contracting:
- Rapid Prototyping services
- New material development
- New metal AM powder
    i. Metal Powder Characterization – providing quality powders for research and material development for metal AM industry.
    ii. Metal AM manufacturing – primarily powder bed and Direct Energy Deposition
- Machining to Support Metal Additive Manufacturing. Precision machining services to complement additive manufacturing processes.
- Metrology Support. Ensure high standards of measurement and quality control. (Partnership with Sandia National Laboratories – National Institute of Standards and Technology (NIST)

C. Manufacturing Training Facility through a contract with ANEW Renewables
- Injection Molding.

- CNC (machining
- Wind Turbines. Manufacturing wind turbines to support the Navajo Nation's sustainable energy master plan.

D. Manufacturing of Metal AM Machines

- A partnership between Ridgeline Manufacturing and Navajo Technical University have used Artificial Intelligence to develop controllers that advance AM machining unique to the AM industry. NAME will be bridging research and grant projects at NTU by bringing the new controllers to the commercialized international market.

E. Metrology/Calibration Lab Contract with Sandia National Laboratories.

- Lab Setup. Sandia National Laboratories and NTU will establish a local metrology/calibration lab to manage overflow work within NAM's operations.
- Certification. The lab will be certified under Sandia's umbrella.
- Services. Electrical calibration and Comprehensive metrology services.

Overall Marketing Prospectus

3D printing will potentially have a greater impact globally over the next 20 years than all the innovations from the industrial revolution combined. Although traditional manufacturing will likely still hold a place in the competitive landscape in the years to come, the next 10 to 20 years promise to reveal a rapid increase in the innovations made possible by 3D printing. The private sector will want to continue working towards embracing this technology as a platform to create new businesses, business models, products and services. The market for rapid prototyping is forecast at $1,496.7 million by 2028.

The global **metrology services** market is anticipated to reach $939.3 million by 2025, according to a new study by Grand View Research, Inc. Increasing demand among end-users in different industries for precision components with tight-tolerance/low-uncertainty limits such as power generation, electronics, and automotive is anticipated to drive growth. Additionally, technological innovation in the field of metrology is expected to positively impact growth. These advancements further influence growth pattern and stimulate new product and software developments for industry players. Consequently, demand for advanced measurement tools and services are expected to aid manufacturers in competently tapping data such as 3D modeling and measurements.

Non-destructive inspection technologies revenue is expected to increase to $16.66 billion by 2029. The forecast period offers huge growth potential for technologies such as computed tomography, phased array ultrasonic testing, and data management tools, as these techniques are more efficient in terms of deriving accurate results. Not to be confused with Non-Destructive Evaluation (NDE; discussed below) which includes both testing and the evaluation of the results, while Non-Destructive Inspection (NDI) is restricted to testing only. One way to look at the differences is that NDI is used to locate defects in an asset while NDE is used to measuring the size, shape, orientation, and other physical characteristics of the defect on top of locating it. The revenue forecast in 2029 for NDI is $16.66 billion.

Composite Manufacturing consists of two distinct materials which together improve product performance and/or lower production costs. Composite materials are essentially a combination of two or more dissimilar materials that are used together to combine best properties or impart a new set of characteristics that neither of the constituent materials could achieve on their own. Composites offer the economic benefits of lower weight and reduced fabrication costs. Because of this, they are ideal for use in many industries. The composite manufacturing industry market forecast is a growth rate of 6.6% with a revenue forecast of $144.5 billion in 2028.

Ceramic Manufacturing. The term "ceramics" refers to a wide range of products and materials used for an equally wide variety of applications, from commercial uses to the aerospace industry. A ceramic is a material that is neither metallic nor organic. Ceramic manufacturing is the process used to sinter and fabricate ceramic materials into non-metal parts. Ceramics have great thermal properties. They can withstand high temperatures, are good thermal insulators, and do not expand greatly when heated. This makes them excellent thermal barriers for applications that range from lining industrial furnaces to covering the space shuttle to protect it from high reentry temperatures. Ceramics are more than pottery and dishes: clay, bricks, tiles, glass, and cement are probably the best-known examples, but ceramics are also used to make spark plugs, fiber optics, artificial joints, space shuttle tiles, cooktops, race car brakes, micro-positioners, chemical sensors, self-lubricating bearings, body armor, and skis to name a variety of productions in various industries. The revenue forecast for ceramics in 2028 is $348.0 billion.

Non-Destructive Evaluation/Testing is a technology which plays a critical role in the safety of the many products, transportation systems, and infrastructure used around the world. The importance of NDE/NDT cannot be overstated as the many applications lead to avoiding catastrophic failures on a daily occurrence. Beyond the important aspects of safety, NDE/NDT measurements provide an essential validation of the quality of a product and add economic value to the manufacturing process, as well as helping manufacturers avoid the costly effects of a poor-quality product reaching the consumer. NDE/NDT offers reliable and accurate results thus providing a foundational stability in manufacturing and production. Since this testing method does not damage the components, all pieces of equipment and machinery can be tested which can minimize the inaccuracy of test results and any undermined irregularities. NDE/NDT provides the "eyes" so the structural engineer can verify, and validate, that manufacturing has delivered what was designed. In aerospace, structural engineers and designers have the fundamental responsibility in the creation of the overall product. The revenue forecast in 2030 for non-destructive evaluation is $34.1 billion.

Initial Marketing Approach for Each Division

Metal AM Powder Manufacturing and Characterization

Metal AM Powder Characterization is another operational component/division that will be developed to serve the Southwest region of the US and beyond in the Metal AM industry. Currently, there are no small niche powder manufacturers who can create small batches of specialized powder at high quality for metal AM.

The division will have two atomizers to create small high-quality batches of metal AM powders as well as a furnace to create the feedstock needed to create new alloyed material.

Academic partners and research will be a large component of this division and will benefit from new material development to be used potentially in the metal AM division.

Customers will include Los Alamos National Laboratory, Sandia National Laboratories and Kansas City Nuclear Security Campus to name a few.

Characterization of metal AM powders will also be a large component to ensure the quality of metal AM powder is of the highest quality.

Metal AM Printing

The metal AM printing operation will work with customers to create prototypes. Prototyping for customers is a low volume high value operation that is needed for the automotive, aerospace and growing space industry. With the New Mexico Space Port growing in customers, the local space industry will need to continue to develop new parts for their applications.

Academic partnerships – Academia needs industry partnerships to conduct relevant research needed for industry. By working with a diverse collection of institutions the business will benefit from new discoveries to gain a competitive edge over the competition.

No less than two metal AM printing machines will be located at the facility to fulfill the contracts.

A partnership will maintain the coordination of activities with the NTU Center for Advanced Manufacturing (CAM) for services not yet housed within the business such as CT scanning, material testing, machining work, etc. Although, it is expected that the business will on board frequently used technologies for manufacturing (Inspection, Non-Destructive Evaluation (NDE), etc.) This will benefit the NTU CAM through generating revenue from industry.

Injection Molding and Machining

ANEW Renewables is a vertical windmill manufacturing company that needs thousands of parts that utilize the injection molding technology. A division of the business will be creating parts for ANEW as well as training new manufacturers to keep up with demand.

Machining for injection molding – machining new dies for injection molding will also be an activity undertaken by this division.

A 5-Axis machining center will be on site as well as a line for injection molding and inspection.

Sandia National Laboratory Electronics Calibration Center

Sandia National Laboratory will be locating a "division" under SNL in partnership with NAM to take on overflow work in electronics calibration. This division will be providing SNL the workspace and personnel to fulfill contracts. Training will be initially provided by SNL.

Certification of the lab will fall under SNL and maintained as a division of SNL.

Initial Equipment and Instrumentation to Be Installed, Phase 1

Metal AM Powder and Characterization
- Two – ATO metal powder atomizers
- Various characterization equipment to be relocated or duplicated from the CAM
- Various characterization equipment

Injection Molding and Machining
- Haitian Dual Screw Extruder System for plastic molding
- 5-Axis Machining Center – machining molds
- Zeiss Vision inspection System

Metal AM Printing

- SLM 2.8 Dual Laser metal AM Powder Bed Laser Fusion System (Funding from State of New Mexico Technology Enhancement Fund to support research projects)

- Farsoon 273M metal AM powder bed laser fusion system (funding from NSF Grant) Will operate in coordination with NTU's CAM
- Metrology Equipment (Faro Arm or equator CMM)
- General Metrology Tools

Other Equipment to be Utilized in Phase 1

- NSI X3000 225 CT Scanner
- Makino U6 Wire EDM
- HAAS VF3SS Machining Center
- Materials Testing Equipment (Fatigue and Tensile Testing equipment)
- Materials Characterization (Zeiss SEM, Microscopy prep equipment)

Phase 1 Workforce: 12-15 estimated. Also interns, trainees, and apprentices
Within five years we are hoping to employ over 100 workers.

Market Prospectus: Powder Manufacturing for Metal AM

First Development of NAME

The current volume of sales for Powder Manufacturing for Metal AM is estimated to be in the range of several hundred million dollars annually. As Metal AM grows as a component of the overall manufacturing sector in the U.S., analysts are projecting a compound annual growth rate (CAGR) of around 15-20%. Further advancements in technology may increase that CAGR

Metal AM Powder Manufacturing and Characterization

Metal AM Powder Characterization is another operational component/division that will be developed to serve the Southwest region of the US and beyond in the Metal AM industry. Currently, there are no small niche powder manufacturers who can create small batches of specialized powder at high quality for metal AM.

The division will have two atomizers to create small high-quality batches of metal AM powders as well as a furnace to create the feedstock needed to create new alloyed material.

Academic partners and research will be a large component of this division and will benefit from new material development to be used potentially in the metal AM division.

Characterization of metal AM powders will also be a large component to ensure the quality of metal AM powder is of the highest quality.

Customer Base

- o Long-term
  - National laboratories like Sandia National Laboratories, Los Alamos National Laboratory, Kansas City Nuclear Security Campus and Idaho National Laboratory.
  - Research institutions focused on material science and engineering advancements.
  - Aerospace companies looking for lightweight components and materials development in metal alloys
  - Automotive Manufacturers seeking complex geometries for parts
  - Medical device manufacturers needing custom implants
- o Initial targets for sales
  - Navajo Technical University's Advanced Manufacturing Lab
  - Sandia National Laboratory
  - Los Alamos National Laboratory
  - Kansas City Nuclear Security Campus

- - Department of Defense
  - University of New Mexico
  - Ridgeland Manufacturing
  - New Mexico State University
  - Virginia Tech
  - Rowan University
  - University of Nebraska
  - New Mexico Tech University
- Current Major Players in the Powder Manufacturing Sector
  - Höganäs AB
  - Carpenter Technology Corporation
  - Arcam AB (a GE company)
  - EOS GmbH.
  - Linde Advanced Materials
  - Reade Advanced Materials
  - Emerging players in the metal powder manufacturing sector include companies like Velo3D, Desktop Metal, and 3D Systems. These companies are gaining traction by focusing on innovative powder formulations and advanced additive manufacturing processes that cater to niche markets and specific applications.

Navajo Advanced Manufacturing Enterprise's Placement in the Market

- - There are no major players in the powder manufacturing sector in the southwest currently. Relationships with Sandia Laboratories, Arizona State University, and Navajo Technical University's Advanced

Manufacturing Laboratory will result in innovations designed to give NAME an entryway into the market that is unique.

Key Initial Benchmarks

- o Installation of equipment already owned into a properly configured powder manufacturing facility
- o Initial production runs to helps set pricing structure
- o Securing of supply of metals appropriate for the making of powder
- o Achieving certification from Sandia Laboratories and NIST
- o Hiring of a Sales Manager
- o Initial sales to the Center for Advanced Manufacturing and Sandia
- o Achieving minority business status from the Small Business Administration
- o Achieving certification as a federal supplier from the General Services Administration and the Defense Logistics Agency
- o Implementation of the marketing plan
- Major Tradeshow for Marketing Powder Manufacturing for Metal AM
  - o Formnext, RAPID + TCT, AMUG Conference (Additive Manufacturing Users Group), and the International Conference on Additive Manufacturing Technologies (AM Tech)

CHAPTER 10

History of and Plans for a Navajo Medical School

The intention of NTU to establish a Navajo Medical School are still in the planning stages. The need for such a medical school dedicated to serving the Navajo people and other American Indian tribes in the southwest and the rest of the United States has been critical for a long period of time. The history of the Navajo Nation's efforts to create such a medical school demonstrates that fact. Since NTU is the leading research university among the TCUs in the nation, the plans for the medical school development envision an institution not only dedicated to treating the people in its primary service area but that will also concentrate research efforts on medical conditions negatively impacting American Indians nationally. A full understanding of traditional approaches to medicine and treatment will inform the application of contemporary modalities in the medical school's curriculum and approaches to treating Native populations.

The first step in creating a medical school was taken when NTU created a pre-med program and built the current chemistry and biology labs in Crownpoint, NM. After installing these labs, duplicate labs were installed in the new classroom building on the Chinle campus. The anticipation is that the original students for the medical school will come from the pre-med program NTU currently has in place. However, NTU will also invite other tribal college students from TCUs across the United States to apply as well as other students transferring into the program from mainstream universities. American Indian students will be encouraged to apply from these universities, but, as is true of NTU's engineering programs, any student will be able to apply for admission since an open admissions policy is in place.

Drs. Elmer Guy and Jason Arviso, NTU's President and Vice President respectively, have worked with the Window Rock School District to secure land for the Medical School campus in property located just over the Arizona-New Mexico border in New Mexico but is adjacent to the school district's land where it has a high school. This property is undeveloped currently but is located close to the *Tséhootsooí* Medical Center operated by the Navajo Nation in Fort Defiance, Arizona.

The plan is to first develop a small campus on this property dedicated to an allied health curriculum that both high school and others interested in a health care career can enroll in as students. This development will trigger a fund-raising effort to create a full-fledged medical school offering both degrees and a research agenda. The plans call for the *Tséhootsooí* Medical Center to provide a place for medical interns and experiential opportunities for students through a partnership between Navajo Nation owned organizations, NTU, and the hospital.

Early discussions have also been held with medical schools in Arizona and New Mexico, asking if they would be willing to partner with NTU in the long-term effort, offering distance education for courses that would not be available during the launch period of the new medical school. These discussions have been based upon research into some of the rural medical school efforts that have successfully been implemented by the University of Kansas and other medical schools around the country dedicated to training physicians and medical personnel for rural America where the shortage of medical professionals is nearly as severe as it is for American Indian nations.[22]

Historical Efforts to Create a Medical School for the Navajo Nation

In 1971, the Navajo Tribal Council suggested that an important component of the solution to the health crises on the Navajo Reservation in Arizona, New Mexico, and Utah was to build a medical school dedicated to training Navajo doctors and other health professionals. Championed by Taylor McKenzie, the first Navajo medical doctor and surgeon and later Vice President of the Navajo Nation, the idea suggested that Navajo doctors would be more likely to stay on the Reservation throughout their careers and build the trust needed for a long-term solution to the medical crisis that in the 1970s produced the following statistics:

> ...life expectancy was two thirds the national average, and the incidence of infant mortality (1.5 times), diabetes (2 times), suicide (3 times), accidents (4 times), tuberculosis (14 times), gastrointestinal infections (27 times), dysentery (40 times), and rheumatic fever (60 times) also were above the national average.[23]

The Indian Health Service (IHS), as is true today, was having trouble getting physicians to agree to live for anything other than short-term stints on the Reservation, especially more rural parts of the Reservation, to provide health services to the Navajo people. At the time, with the founding of Navajo Community College in 1969, there was an increasing understanding that the best people to solve Navajo problems were Navajos practicing self-determination. This applied especially to Navajo medical professionals who would use their insights into the culture, language, and people to achieve breakthroughs in both medical and health practices grounded in Navajo culture, traditional foods and treatments, and society that would eventually end the centuries-old health challenges that were seemingly intractable.

The effort to build a medical school was stalled when funding could not be secured from Congress or other sources.

The Current Proposal for NTU to Create a Medical School

The current proposal to create a medical school that serves not only Navajo but also other American Indian people came about when the Navajo Nation Vice President, Rex Lee Jim, asked the President and Provost of Navajo Technical College to again take on the challenge of building a medical school[24]. Then, after a new Navajo Nation President and Vice President were elected, the new President asked Navajo Tech to continue the effort.

There are just under 400,000 Navajo tribal members. The university serves, in addition to this population, several Pueblo and Ute tribal communities, as well as off-

Reservation communities in New Mexico and Arizona. It is built around three themes: STEM, health, and trades programs, all anchored in a mission that emphasizes Navajo cultural values. The Navajo Medical School will also be designed to serve students from all American Indian nations who want to serve their people as well as non-Indians interested in a career in Indian country.

Navajo Tech is one of the most successful minority serving institutions of higher learning in the nation in terms of delivering academically rigorous curriculum while achieving higher retention and graduation rates with American Indian students than institutions of higher learning located in its service area.

The need for the creation of a medical school that serves not only the Navajo people but all Indian people living in the U.S. rests partially in the fact that several substantial efforts to improve Indian health outcomes have not succeeded. The incidence of individual diseases may have changed. For instance, in 1971 tuberculosis was one of the deadliest problems for Indian people nationwide. Today tuberculosis is still a serious problem that needs to be addressed, but its incidence has gone down on a per 100,000 population bases. Certainly, technology and the advancement in treating several diseases have helped American Indians as well as the U.S. population in general.

Still, American Indians have the greatest health challenges of any demographic population in the U.S. When IHS was made a separate agency in 1955 out of the Bureau of Indian Affairs, some improvements in overall health for Indian people were achieved. Additional hospitals, clinics and health centers (today there are 33 hospitals, 59 health centers, and 50 health stations) improved access and the ability to treat illness and other medical challenges found on reservations. Yet, the overall scope of the problem of

Indian health has not changed. In fact, a 2010 report by the Senate Committee on Indian Affairs found that in the Aberdeen region (which covers 18 tribes in North and South Dakota, Nebraska, and Iowa), the IHS is in a chronic state of crisis.[25] There is evidence the same is true of the other regions served by the IHS, including the southwest.

The need has grown with passage of the Affordable Care Act. Since Indian Nations tend to be centers of poverty throughout the nation, the percentage of the population affected by the Act is higher than in many of the more prosperous parts of the country. With a greater part of the population now covered by health insurance, the need for General Practice Physicians has grown. Still, the number of American Indian physicians is extremely low compared to other demographic populations.

As an article by Rivo and Kindig in the *New England Journal of Medicine* reported, "The number of medical school graduates from underrepresented minority groups increased between 1988 and 1994, from 1,345 to 1,495, or from 7.8 to 8.6 percent of the total number..."26 but falls far short of the numbers needed to reflect the percentage of each minority group in the overall population. This shortage exacerbates the shortage of physicians willing to practice as General Practitioners in rural areas with large minority problems:

> In a 1992 report, the Council on Graduate Medical Education concluded that deficiencies in the physician work force, the medical-education system, and public policy would hinder efforts to provide high-quality and affordable health care for all people in the United States. A surplus of specialists, shortages of minority physicians and generalists, poor geographic distribution of physicians, and

inadequate training of physicians in key practice skills were identified as problems.[27]

On the Navajo Nation not only are there too few physicians to adequately meet the needs of the population, but shortages of doctors and nurses have forced temporary closures of emergency centers in the Navajo Nation in recent years, endangering the health outcomes for scores of community members.

In responding to the Navajo Nation's President and Vice President request to establish a Navajo-based medical school, the university's administrators began exploring what would be needed to start the process by developing an academically rigorous pre-med program. The curriculum necessary to create a pre-med program was developed and is currently in the university catalog. The university has also installed top-flight biology and chemistry labs in both the Crownpoint and Chinle campuses. Pre-med students have earned their undergraduate degree from Navajo Tech and been admitted to medical programs at Harvard and other medical schools.

Current planning, which has continued through a change of Navajo Nation leadership, would create a medical school that serves not only Southwestern Indian Tribes but would also encourage recruitment of students from other tribal colleges and universities (TCUs) in the U.S. There are 32 accredited TCUs found in Alaska, the West, Southwest, and Midwest. This means that graduates from the school would tend to go back to their home Native Nations and serve the people there that are consistently underserved. Students would also be recruited from rural areas around the Navajo Nation in New Mexico, Arizona, Utah, and Colorado.

The Health Disparities Between American Indians and the Rest of the American Population

An AI search, using ChatGPT, shows the disparity between the health outcomes for American Indians vs. the rest of the American population. This disparity provides the strongest possible rationale for the creation of a Navajo Medical School. As Taylor McKenzie indicated all those years ago, one of the challenges in providing quality medical services to American Indian communities is to attract quality professional to those communities, many of which are in isolated regions.

IHS has faced challenges in this respect for all its existence. This is one of the reasons IHS has struggled to improve the health outcomes for American Indian people. Too often contractors are hired, costing the American taxpayer high fees, who provide services for a short period of time, never really getting to know their patients or their medical needs or history, and then move on to their next contract assignment. As the old saying goes, that is no way to build a railroad, or a successful health system.

Health Disparity Data

The health disparities between American Indians (AI) and the general American population are significant and multifaceted. Below are key statistics and factors that illustrate these disparities:

1. Life Expectancy
   - American Indians: The average life expectancy for American Indians is approximately 73 years.
   - U.S. Population: The life expectancy for the general U.S. population is around 79 years.

- Disparity: This represents a difference of about 6 years, with American Indians having a notably lower life expectancy.

2. Chronic Diseases

- Diabetes:
    - Prevalence: The prevalence of diabetes among American Indians is about 16.1%, compared to approximately 7.4% in the general U.S. population.
- Obesity:
    - Rate: About 39% of American Indians are classified as obese, compared to 31% of the overall American population.
- Heart Disease: American Indians experience higher rates of heart disease and are more than twice as likely to die from heart disease compared to white Americans.

3. Mental Health

- Suicide Rates: The suicide rate among American Indians is twice the national average, with young American Indians (ages 15-24) facing particularly high rates.
- Substance Abuse: American Indians have higher rates of substance abuse disorders, with alcohol-related deaths being significantly higher than the national average.

4. Access to Healthcare

- Health Insurance Coverage: Roughly 30% of American Indians do not have health insurance, compared to around 8% of the overall U.S. population.
- Indian Health Service (IHS): The IHS, which provides healthcare to American Indians, is significantly

underfunded, resulting in limited access to services and longer wait times for care.

5. Infant Mortality
- The infant mortality rate for American Indians is 10.5 per 1,000 live births, compared to 5.6 per 1,000 live births for the general U.S. population, indicating higher risks during pregnancy and childbirth.

6. Cancer Rates
- Certain types of cancer, such as lung and colorectal cancer, are more prevalent among American Indians. For instance, American Indian men have higher rates of lung cancer than the national average.

7. Preventable Conditions
- Diseases such as hypertension and chronic respiratory diseases are more common among American Indians, contributing to higher rates of morbidity and mortality.

Key Factors Contributing to Disparities

1. Socioeconomic Status: Many American Indian communities face high levels of poverty, which limits access to healthcare, healthy food, and education.
2. Geographic Barriers: Many American Indians live in rural areas with limited access to healthcare facilities and providers.
3. Cultural Factors: There are cultural differences in health beliefs and practices that affect health-seeking behavior and the effectiveness of healthcare delivery.

4. Historical Trauma: The legacy of colonization, forced relocation, and systemic discrimination has long-term impacts on mental and physical health.[28]

Conclusion

The health disparities between American Indians and the general U.S. population are stark, with significant gaps in life expectancy, prevalence of chronic diseases, mental health outcomes, and access to healthcare. Addressing these disparities requires a multifaceted approach that considers the socioeconomic, cultural, and historical contexts affecting American Indian communities.

Creation of a Navajo Medical School by NTU, a university that has already proven its ability to create extraordinary programs in STEM fields and health, including engineering, technology, and Counseling in Crisis Management and Suicide Prevention and in Substance Abuse Disorder provides an important way to address what has been an historical failure by the United States government.

By creating an increasingly larger number of health professionals concentrating on American Indian health issues, an opportunity exists to not only increase the number of doctors and nurses willing to live and serve long-term in Native communities but to also increase the understanding of Native problems, concerns, history, language, culture, and the psychological needs of the individuals in those communities by those professionals. As the medical workforce increases, the chances for significant innovations and the application of innovations both developed by this workforce and the world's medical ecosystem also increases.

A Navajo medical school will also be willing to use traditional Native approaches to healing and understand that projects like the NEXUS award winning project developed by the Environmental Science faculty and students that emphasizes the health benefits of Native foods are important in treating Native American health challenges. As Dr. Mackenzie argued so many years ago, American Indian people want to be in their communities. They are not outsiders to the culture and the lifestyles of the people they serve.

By training medical professionals in a medical school managed by Navajo, or other tribal, doctors and nurses,[29] a larger number of medical professions will be dedicated for all their careers to solve some of the problems that have plagued Native American health outcomes for so long. In the modern world, one of the biggest challenges of the IHS is to find physicians that will be comfortable living in American Indian communities. Too often those who do serve in such rural, culturally rich places, only stay for short periods and then move on to the rest of their careers in communities where they feel more comfortable.

A Navajo medical school is the most practical solution to that problem. American Indians will succeed, as they do at TCUs in general, at a higher rate than they do in mainstream medical schools. This will create a stream of qualified American Indian professionals that will spread out across the country, providing an important solution to the dilemma of American Indian health outcomes. The challenge will be to convince both the government, private foundations, and the Navajo Nation to participate in the effort.

C H A P T E R   1 1

Chemistry and the NEST Lab

By Thiagarajan Soundappan

Dr. Soundappan, third from left, and students in the NEST Lab

Out of the 34 TCUs in the United States, NTU is the first to offer a Baccalaureate of Science (B.S.) degree in

Chemistry. Dr. Thiagrarajan Soundappan collaborated with external academic partners (Harvard, Arizona State University, and Washington State University) to design a curriculum balancing a research agenda with academic rigor and cultural relevance. The research agenda developed incorporated advanced electrochemistry research, which led to the creation of the Nanoelectrochemical Analysis and Energy Storage Laboratory (NEST Lab) on the Crownpoint campus.

The NEST Lab is primarily used by students to conduct research in areas such as sensors and energy storage. Batteries and sensors are becoming increasingly important aspects of the contemporary world, important in the energy, automobile, technology, and even medical economic sectors. By creating opportunities for hands-on research in these areas, students become eligible to join graduate programs at various institutions, creating a technological bridge connecting the classroom to the broader scientific community. There is also an expectation that research and collaborations at NTU will one day lead to economic opportunities on the Navajo Nation that will lead to high skill, high knowledge, high wage careers located on the Reservation.

Dr. Soundappan's research has focused on developing innovative materials for electrochemical sensors, batteries, and supercapacitors. These technologies are critical for renewable energy systems, especially in off-grid and rural environments like the Navajo Nation. His work has explored materials with enhanced energy storage capacity, durability, and environmental compatibility. By working with students to further and expand research in such areas, Soundappan and NTU are attempting to utilize the results of this work to meet the urgent energy needs of indigenous communities throughout the U.S. Results from the work will also be applicable to many other rural, isolated communities in this country and in other parts of the world.

Several goals are embedded into the design of the NTU Chemistry program and the NEST Lab. First, NTU has grown from a regional technical university into a nationally recognized university in STEM education and research. Second, several students have been admitted into graduate programs in institutions like Harvard based on their academic preparation and research skills. Third, the NEST Lab particularly is laying the groundwork for young Navajo entrepreneurs and even the eventual creation of an eventual Navajo industry centered around electrochemical sensors, batteries, and supercapacitors. Fourth, the program and lab establish a model that other TCUs and minority-serving institutions of higher learning can follow to create a larger presence of American Indians in chemistry-related fields.

The last aspect of what has been achieved by the chemistry program is that culturally relevant science education has been organized for Navajo youth through annual science fairs, hands-on science workshops, and classroom presentations. This work is helping to inspire young students to break the glass ceiling and become scientists that can transform their communities and reshape global science.

Artificial Intelligence (AI) at NTU

NTU started making efforts to develop projects in Artificial Intelligence (AI) relatively early in the current AI era. Tom Davis, former Provost of the university, was the President of a software development company early in his career, where he and his programmers tried to use what was then known about AI to develop automated layout software for the publication industry. The effort was not fully successful, although they came out with a product that was used in a few small newspapers, but he kept in touch what was going on with AI throughout his years as an educator.

Short History of AI Development

AI has, of course, evolved over several decades. In the 1940s and 50s, some of the early concepts were developed, including work by Alan Turing, the British inventor of the first computer, the Bombe machine, used in deciphering German Enigma code messages that helped win World War II. The Dartmouth Conference in 1956 is often considered the birth of artificial intelligence as a field. At that conference key figures like John McCarthy, Marvin Minsky, Claude Shannon and Herbert Simon proposed that a machine could be built that could exhibit aspects of human intelligence.

From the 50s to the 1970s the first AI programs, such as Logic Theorist and General Problem Solver, were developed. Symbolic AI research centered around symbolic reasoning and problem-solving, and this led to the development of LISt Processing (LISP) and other languages developed specifically for AI programming.

Unfortunately, these early efforts were not successful at handling what at the time was called "real-world complexity," and funding for research in AI plummeted. In the early 1980s, when Tom Davis was the President of Synaptic Micro Solutions, a revival of AI ensued with the development of what were called "expert systems" like MYCIN, developed at Stanford University to assist in diagnosing and treating bacterial infections. These systems used rule-based approaches that tried to mimic human expertise in specific knowledge areas such as engineering design and financial services, as well as layout of newspapers and other forms of publication, a project undertaken by the firm Davis headed.

Then there were dramatic advances in both computational hardware and algorithms. Neural networks consisting of connected units, or nodes, were developed that somewhat mirrored the way nodes, or synapses, in the brain work. Backward chaining algorithms allowed multi-layered networks to create functions that had not been feasible in the past. Machine learning algorithms shifted the focus from the old rule-based approaches to data-driven approaches. This effectively laid the groundwork for contemporary AI.

From the 1990s to the 2010s, large datasets propagated throughout the world of commerce. Improved algorithms, partially designed by big corporations seeking increasingly more advanced ways for identifying customers and making product advancements, led to breakthroughs in machine learning. Speech recognition, natural language processing, and computer vision and imaging were all products rising from these breakthroughs. Then the deep learning revolution began to revolutionize all computational science.

Today generative AI is generating human-like text and images, resulting in products used by everyday people like ChatGPT or virtual assistants like Siri and Alexa. The next revolution in AI is also in process. The Turing Award in 2025 went to two researchers, one in the U.S., the other in Canada, that worked on reinforcement learning, basically taking the idea of the pain/pleasure learning response in humans and animals and training computer systems to "learn" like humans by reinforcing right/wrong responses to different scenarios or problems. Right becomes analogous to the pleasure response; a wrong response becomes analogous to a pain response within the AI software

Now the idea of "chain of thought" reasoning is at the forefront of AI research. The idea, like the idea of reinforcement learning, is straightforward. Instead of just using reinforcement learning to develop a "reasoning" system, developing a logically connected sequence of steps, or logic train, to solve a problem, computation can sort through massive numbers of what/if scenarios at blinding speed. In Reasoning AI, the algorithms are used to develop a logic-train that applies a solution to a specific problem or scenario and then runs through scenarios to arrive at an optimum solution. Not only can a system learn, but it can also reason, providing a new level of solutions to complex problems and dilemmas.

NTU's Involvement in the AI Revolution

In 1986 the National Center for Supercomputing Applications (NCSA) was established at the University of Illinois at Urbana Champaign through major funding from the National Science Foundation (NSF). Larry Smarr, the principal investigator (PI), began inviting other colleges and universities, including TCUs, to join in the national effort to push supercomputing to increasing levels of performance.

Tom Davis and Mark Trebian, who would later join NTU as a faculty member, represented the TCUs in this effort. Dr. Smarr's work at the University of Illinois paved the way for the development of the early World Wide Web, contributing to the creation of the first web server and web browsers, and then for high performance computing developments, including AI. For decades Davis, Trebian, and others at NTU like Jared Ribble and Jason Arviso attended Supercomputing (SC) conferences located around the country and were involved in various projects and research efforts undertaken in partnership with members of NCSA.

Just one example of this effort was the creation of a mini-computer lab at NTU that linked together various workstations in the lab to create a high-performance computing environment so that students could be introduced to advanced concepts and skills associated with computational thinking, visualization walls, and various efforts in creating networks designed to further research collaborations, including the transfer of large files for real-time access by multiple researchers over distance. Jared Ribble, the IT Director, worked with Trebian and the students to take what was being learned in the classroom and create projects related to campus networking, visualization, and cybersecurity.

As AI applications began appearing at SC conferences, efforts to utilize AI at NTU were introduced. The first efforts were attempted in the Center for Advanced Manufacturing where Scott Halliday started exploring how AI was likely to impact Advance Manufacturing in four areas: educating students for high skill, high wage jobs in the field, improving the performance of Metal AM machines through the development of an AI-enabled controller, utilizing metrology to ensure exacting quality standards, and in creating metal composites that meet performance requirements for parts manufactured through Metal AM processes. There was also discussion about how AI was likely to impact manufacturing processes, especially as AI Reasoning, which was then being talked about but not implemented, might impact the production of parts, products, and quality control.

NTU was also experiencing challenges in its financial department, causing audit and processing dilemmas. Concerned, President Guy talked to Harshwal & Company, LLC, a firm the university had worked with for several years, that had AI programmers on staff. NTU asked for several AI-enabled products designed to help improve accounting processes based upon its understanding of AI, and Harshwal delivered the first product automating the processing of Indirect Cost so that NTU could field test it. Since then, several other projects have been started and are in the process of implementation, improving NTU's ability to operate its financial department at a highly professional level.

In consultation with the Department of Defense, the university launched a cybersecurity program it is offering to students. It also assigned one of NTU's most experience IT technicians to concentrate on cybersecurity. At the current time, AI is impacting cybersecurity at an increasingly rapid pace, and NTU is working hard to keep up with those developments.

Plans Concerning AI

The current effort in AI at NTU is extensive. Not all the efforts underway at the university can be covered in this short chapter. Many of the efforts still need to secure funding to go forward. But a small sample of the ideas shows just how extensive the thought and efforts are.

Plans are underway to hire a new AI expert to develop new curriculum in AI. This curriculum will be made available to students in Computer Science and Information Technology but also to students in fields like Advanced Manufacturing, Electrical Engineering, Environmental Science, and Chemistry. These new employees will also be asked to work with faculty to develop a research agenda that enhances both skills and knowledge about AI as it applies to each content area and then help implement that agenda.

This design is modeled on what NTU has achieved with its Center for Advanced Manufacturing. AI is going to impact nearly every field of endeavor as universities, labs, individuals, and businesses create new applications. NTU plans to strengthen its IT and Computer Science programs, but it also wants to help other disciplines achieve breakthroughs that can benefit the Navajo people in their respective fields. NTU is working with the State of New Mexico to implement this project.

Brief descriptions of AI projects being pursued at NTU are as follows:

AI for manufacturing

Microstructure/Parameter correlation:

For metal additive manufacturing, there is a need to connect parameter settings to microstructures. This means that there are certain properties we want to create from the metal additive manufacturing process. Changing those properties and changing the cooling rate creates different microstructures, thus changing the material's physical properties. Through AI, these connections cannot only be made but can be optimized, resulting in superior products created through Metal AI processes. This work in AI could strengthen the promise of Advanced Manufacturing to the regional economy of the Southwest as well as the national economy.

Parameter optimization:

Another metal AM application is to create a correlation between parameter settings and porosity, or quality, of the part being created. Prediction is a large part of getting to the optimum solution quickly. There are new materials being developed in the form of alloys (which is another AI application). The parameters of these alloys need to be quickly determined and then dialed in. Currently, the metal AM world takes a lot of time to "perfect" a part. By using AI to develop correlations, determinations can be sped up and the effectiveness of using novel alloys to meet specific product needs and specifications can become a significant aspect of the "perfection" process.

Tutor on the Shoulder:

Together with New Collar Network, NTU is working on online help, tutoring, and teaching modules that utilize AI for not only training but as an interactive help desk. There are some basic rules of thumb with metal AM that transcend machines and very machine specific applications. AI can do the searching for what the trainee or operator is asking much faster and more accurately than searching through manuals or trying to get answers from experts that are often not readily available.

AI is data driven, and machines can feed data to AI to solve almost any need including metrology, process optimization, material usage and design optimization/iterations. These tools provide a new dimension to what will be possible in manufacturing.

IT Infrastructure and AI

NTU has been involved with high performance computing (HPC) and new technologies it enables since the beginning of the NCSA, as described earlier. Several partners are working with NTU on these efforts. Some of the projects being implemented or explored in HPC and networked systems are as follows:

AI-Powered Network Automation & Optimization

This project is designed to integrate AI automation into our college's "white box" network infrastructure, enabling dynamic traffic management, self-healing network configurations, and intelligent load balancing. The system will learn from traffic patterns and use machine learning algorithms to analyze them and learn to adjust network parameters autonomously, without human intervention. Funding will go towards developing the AI model, upgrading the hardware and implementing the SDN.

AI-Driven Network Security & Threat Detection

As the cyber threat continues to evolve, traditional security measures often fail to provide real time anomaly detection. To this end, this project is a proposal for implementing an Intrusion Detection System (IDS) with AI power, which uses machine learning to monitor, detect and control cyber threats in real time in our white box switch infrastructure. The model will monitor traffic logs and, based on what is identified as not normal, will alert the user of possible security breaches and generate a response to the threats. The grant funding will go towards the development of the AI, the creation of training datasets, and the interface with the current network monitoring tools.

Edge AI & Software-Defined Networking (SDN) Integration

In a software defined white box networking environment, this project will use AI integrated edge computing to design a smart self-optimizing campus network. It will learn from data processed at the edge using AI algorithms, looking at real time network performance, routing, and bandwidth adjustment. The system will enhance latency critical applications of IoT based smart campus solutions, AI enabled classrooms, and research computing. Funding will be used for AI software development, acquiring edge computing hardware and implementing SDN.

Energy-Efficient Edge AI Cluster for Smart Campus Applications

This project will create an AI edge computing cluster that processes real-time IoT data on campus. The system will be supported by low power edge devices such as NVIDIA Jetson or Raspberry Pi clusters and support applications like smart lighting, intelligent traffic monitoring and predictive building maintenance. The AI will improve the energy efficiency and thus the cost and carbon footprint. Funding will be used for hardware procurement, AI development, and integration with the campus IoT infrastructure.

Student-Driven AI Cluster for Open Source and Community Research

This project will build a low-cost AI cluster on commodity hardware, off the shelf components, and open-source software such as TensorFlow, PyTorch, Apache Spark to enable student led AI research. The cluster will also be open to local nonprofits and small businesses, so students can apply their learning to real world AI tasks. The funding will be used for server purchase, student training to use the servers and work on the projects and for collaboration with local businesses.

AI-Enhanced Network Monitoring & Cybersecurity Cluster

Cyber threats are increasing, and conventional monitoring tools are failing to provide real time detection of cyber-attacks. In this project, a dedicated AI based cybersecurity cluster will be developed to identify network anomalies, phishing attempts, and intrusion patterns in real time using machine learning models. The cluster will analyze real time campus network traffic, log data and security incidents and raise automated alerts and adaptive firewall responses. Funding will be used for computing nodes, AI security model development and integration with white box networking.

AI-Based Wireless Intrusion Detection and Security System

Cyber-attacks on wireless networks include unauthorized access, spoofing and denial of service attacks. In this project, an AI enabled wireless intrusion detection (WIDS) system will be implemented to monitor the network traffic, identify anomalies and block possible security threats on auto pilot. The system will also leverage past incidents to improve the accuracy of its detection. Funding will support AI cybersecurity development, acquisition of network monitoring hardware, and software integration.

AI-Powered Wireless Mesh Network for Disaster Resilience

During natural disasters or network failures, reliable communication is crucial. This project will develop an AI-powered wireless mesh network that can automatically reconfigure itself when certain access points go offline. AI will predict potential network failures and reroute traffic before disruptions occur.

Several of these projects involve graduate students in Electrical Engineering. They are partnering with NTU's IT Director in pursuing them.

Conclusion

NTU has a long history is pursuing projects developed out of the high-performance computing efforts kicked into high gear by the formation of the NCSA, which members of NTU's faculty and staff were involved in when the organization was founded. Over the years, several projects that have garnered national attention flowed from NTU's projects relating to computational science. The IT and Computer Science degrees at NTU have generated an American Indian workforce as sophisticated and competent as that coming out of major universities.

Efforts to create AI research that can lead to economic development for the Navajo and Zuni Pueblo people has been increasing in intensity at NTU during the last five years. Efforts to utilize AI, and create products and processes in AI, particularly in Advanced Manufacturing and accounting have already resulted in the ability to work more efficiently in some cases and to create important intellectual property in others. This is expected to continue to develop as NTU moves into a future where AI in areas like cybersecurity, computation, Advanced Manufacturing, and even Environmental Science continues to become increasingly vital. NTU is working on training, coursework, degrees, and research to ensure the Navajo and Zuni people and the institution itself is not left behind during the ongoing AI revolution.

One aspect of what NTU is doing that is unique is that the work in AI is not relegated to disciplines but is cross-disciplinary.

Courses in AI can be utilized in different degree fields, and employees in the process of being hired will be assigned to work not only in Information Science and Computer Science but also with students, professors, and instructors in other fields wishing to pursue projects and research in AI.

The biggest challenge currently is to expand funding for the work in AI at the university. The good news is that NTU is used to doing research on the "bleeding edge" of STEM that can lead to economic development long-term for not only the Navajo people but all the people in the states where the university has campuses or instructional sites.

CHAPTER 13

NTU 2024 Publications

Dr. Guy's push to create a strong Navajo research agenda at NTU has resulted in years of peer reviewed publications. A good illustration of this accomplishment comes from those publications authored by faculty and students and appearing in peer reviewed journals or books during 2024. NTU authors are highlighted in bold. This is also a good example of some of the partnerships by university faculty and administrators have developed throughout the United States. It also serves as indicator for just how accomplished the university is at achieving its long-term goals since this effort took over a decade to come to full fruition.

Chatue, I. A.D., Nyegue1, M.A. Kamdem, S.D., **Maloba, F.**, Junaid, T.I., Malhotra, P., **Netongo, P.M**. (2024). Association between Epstein-Barr virus reactivation and severe malaria in pregnant women living in a malaria-endemic region of Cameroon. *PLOS Global Public Health* https://doi.org/10.1371/journal.pgph.0003556

Davis, Thomas. Juniper's Dragon. 2/29/2024. Novel: Four Windows Press.

Ehsan Dehghan-Niri, Nihar Masurkar, Hamidreza Nemati, Zachary Goode, **Harold Scott Halliday** and Juergen

Liebig. Overcoming Challenges in the Biomimetic Study of Termite Drumming Behavior.

Fogang, B., Schoenhals, M. **Franklin M. Maloba**, F., Biabi, A.F., Essangui, E., Donkeu, C., Cheteug, G., Kapen, M., Keumoe, R., Kemleu, S., Nsango, S.N., Cornwall, D.H., Eboumbou, C., Perraut, R., Megnekou, R., Lamb, T.J., Ayong L.S. (2024). Asymptomatic carriage of Plasmodium falciparum in children living in a hyperendemic area occurs independently of IgG responses but is associated with a balanced inflammatory cytokine ratio. *Malaria Journal* (2024) 23:268. https://doi.org/10.1186/s12936-024-05086-8

Gowdaman, R., Deepa, A., **Singla, Y.K.** (2024). Recent Advances in PVDF/Carbon-Based Nanocomposite Fibers for Piezoelectric Energy Harvesting Applications. *J. Electron. Mater.* 54, 24–50. https://doi.org/10.1007/s11664-024-11589-6

Halder, S., **RoyChowdhury, A.**, Kar, S., Ray, D., Bhandari, G. (2024). Critical Watershed Prioritization through Multi-Criteria Decision-Making Techniques and Geographical Information System Integration for Watershed Management. Sustainability. 2024, 16, 3467. https://doi.org/10.3390/su16083467

Hussen, A., Illafe, M., Zeyani, A., Fekete-Szegö (2024). Second Hankel Determinant for a Certain Subclass of Bi-Univalent Functions associated with Lucas-Balancing Polynomials, *International Journal of Neutrosophic Science 25 (3)*, 417-434. https://doi.org/10.54216/IJNS.250336.

Hussen, A., Madi, M. S. A., Abominjil, A. M. M. (2024). Bounding coefficients for certain subclasses of bi-univalent functions related to Lucas-Balancing polynomials. AIMS *Mathematics 9, no. 7*: 18034-18047

Hussen, A., Alamari, M. M. (2024). Bounds on Coefficients for a Subclass of Bi-Univalent Functions with Lucas-Balancing Polynomials and Rruscheweyh Derivative Operator. *Computer Science 19, no. 4*: 1237-1249

Hussen, A. (2024). An application of the Mittag-Leffler-type Borel distribution and Gegenbauer polynomials on a certain subclass of bi-univalent functions. *Heliyon 10, no. 10.*

Illafe, M., Mohd, M. H., Yousef, F., Supramaniam, S. (2024). Bounds for the second Hankel determinant of a general subclass of bi-univalent functions, *International Journal of Mathematics Engineering and Management Science, 9(5)*, 1226-1239. https://doi.org/10.33889/IJMEMS.2024.9.5.065

Illafe M., Mohd, M. H., Yousef, F., Supramaniam, S. (2024). A Subclass of bi-univalent functions defined by a Symmetric q-derivative operator and Gegenbauer polynomials, *European Journal of Pure and Applied Mathematics, 17(4)*, 2467-2480. https://doi.org/10.29020/nybg.ejpam.v17i4.5408

Illafe, M., Yousef, F., Haji Mohd, M., Supramaniam, S. (2024). Fundamental properties of a class of analytic functions defined by a generalized multiplier transformation operator, *International Journal of Mathematics and Computer Science, 19(4) (2024)*, 1203-1211. https://doi.org/10.1007/s13324-021-00491-7

Illafe, M., Mohd, M. H., Yousef, F., Supramaniam, S. (2024). Investigating Inclusion, Neighborhood, and Partial Sums Properties for a General Subclass of Analytic Functions, *International Journal of Neutrosophic Science 25 (3), 501-510,* https://doi.org/10.54216/IJNS.250341

Joshi, M., Razaur Rahman Shaon, M., **Rezwana, S.**, Wang, K., Zhao, S., Ivan, J., Jackson, E. (2024). Developing a Comprehensive Vulnerable Road User Safety Screening Method Using Multi-Level Data. *Transportation Research Record*, 03611981241254386.

Kar, S., Chowdhury, S., Gupta, T., Hati, D., De, A., Ghatak, Z., Tinab, T., Rahman, I.T., Chatterjee, S., **RoyChowdhury, A**. (2024). A Study on the Impact of Air Pollution on Health Status of Traffic Police Personnel in Kolkata, India. Air. 2024, 2(1), 1-23. https://doi.org/10.3390/air2010001

Kaustubh Deshmukh, Alex Riensche, Ben Bevans, Ryan J. Lane, Kyle Snyder, **Harold (Scott) Halliday**, Christopher B. Williams, Reza Mirzaeifar, Prahalada Rao. Effect of processing parameters and thermal history on microstructure evolution and functional properties in laser powder bed fusion of 316. *Materials & Design* 244 (2024) 113136

Kogularasu S., Sriram Balasubramanian, S., Chang-Chien, G.P., Ahammad, S.U. W., **Billey, W., Platero, J., Soundappan** T., Sekhar P. (2024). Advances in Electrochemical Sensors: Improving Food Safety, Quality, and Traceability *ECS Sensors Plus, Volume 3, Number 2.* **DOI** 10.1149/2754-2726/ad5455

Lin, Q., Lin, Z., Lin, S., Fatmi, Z., Rizvi, N.A., Hussain, M.M., Siddique, A., **Moyebi, O.D.**, Carpenter, D.O., Khwaja, H.A. (2024). Impact of fine particulate pollution exposures on respiratory health in a megacity of Pakistan. *Atmospheric Pollution Research, 5(12).* doi: 10.1016/j.apr.2024.102277

Martinez, C.J., Das, D., Bloomfield, E.F., Abraham, J.D., Knox, J.A., Simmonds, R., Hilderbrand, D.C., Giovannettone, J., Gouw, A.M., **RoyChowdhury, A**. (2024) Bridging the COSMOS: How the inclusion of and collaboration with Faith-based Understandings and Indigenous Knowledges can transform the Weather, Water, and Climate Enterprise. *Bulletin of the American Meteorological Society*, 105, E1734–E1754. https://doi.org/10.1175/BAMS-D-23-0047.1

Mishra, S., Chhibber, R., **Singla, Y. K**. (2024). Effects of CaO–ZrO2–SiO2–CaF2–TiO2-based electrode coating components on weld chemistry and microhardness. *Journal of Materials Research and Technology*, *33*, 8918–8928. https://doi.org/10.1016/j.jmrt.2024.11.179

Sekhar, P. **Billey, W**., **Begay, M**., Thomas, B., **Woody, C**., **Soundappan, T**. (2024). Sensor Reproducibility Analysis: Challenges and Potential Solutions. ECS Sensors plus **DOI** 10.1149/2754-2726/ad9936

Moyebi, O.D., Lebbie, T., Carpenter, D.O. (2024). Standards for levels of lead in soil and dust around the world. *Reviews on Environmental Health*. doi: 10.1515/reveh-2024-0030.

Rezwana, S., Lownes, N. (2024). Interactions and Behaviors of Pedestrians with Autonomous Vehicles: A Synthesis. *Future Transportation, 4(3),* 722-745

Rezwana, S., Shaon, M. R. R., Lownes, N., Jackson, E. (in press). Bridging the gap: Understanding the factors affecting pedestrian safety perceptions in the age of driverless vehicles. *Traffic Safety Research Journal*

Zhang, Z., Satpathy, A., **Morris, K**., **RoyChowdhury, A**., Datta, R., Sarkar, D. (2024) Organic Amendments Improve the Quality of Coal Gob Spoils: A Sustainable Mining Waste Reclamation *Method. Applied Science, 2024, 14,* 9723. https://doi.org/10.3390/app14219723

2024 Conference Proceedings

*Bebo, C., Tibbits, D., Chang, C., *Carver, M., Dimaio, M., RoyChowdhury, A., Olsen, P., Basu, A., Kinney, S. Rapid Quantification of Uranium in Bedrock: A New Framework for Parameterizing Geogenic Contribution to Groundwater Contamination. Geological Society of America 2024 annual meeting. Anaheim, CA (September 22-25, 2024)

Ehsan Dehghan-Niri, Nihar Masurkar, Hamidreza Nemati, Zachary Goode, **Harold Scott Halliday** and Juergen Liebig. Overcoming Challenges in the Biomimetic Study of Termite Drumming Behavior. IEEE ROBIO 2024 conference, Presented by Dr. Niri, https://ieee-robio.org/2024.

Khan, M. T. H., Rezwana, S. Assessing the Sustainability Impacts of Additive Manufacturing: A Review. In International Manufacturing Science and Engineering Conference (Vol. 88100, p. V001T04A011). *American Society of Mechanical Engineers.* (June 2024)

Khan, M. T. H., Rezwana, S. Bridging worlds: The role of indigenous knowledge in engineering education: A literature-based study. *FIE Conference Proceedings of presentation.* Washington, DC. (2024, October)

Martinez, C.J., Das, D., Bloomfield, E.F., Abraham, J.D., Knox, J.A., Simmonds, R., Hilderbrand, D.C., Giovannettone, J., Gouw, A.M., **RoyChowdhury, A**. Bridging the Cosmos: Initiatives from the AMS Committee on Spirituality, Multifaith Outreach, and Science to promote Faith-based Understandings and Indigenous Knowledges in the Geoscience Enterprise. American Geophysical Union (AGU) Fall 2024 Meeting. Washington, D.C. (December 9-13, 2024)

Shekhar, P., **Khan, M. T. H.**, Gajjar, S.). Work in Progress: Utilizing Decision Tree Analysis for Engineering Students' GPA Prediction. In *2024 IEEE World Engineering Education Conference (EDUNINE)* (pp. 1-4). IEEE. (March 2024)

*****Tome, M.**, **RoyChowdhury,** A., *****Wilson, D.**, *Yazzie, T., Frey, B., Yu, J., Sturgis, L., Tsosie, R., Development of an Advanced Membrane Desalination Technology to Address Groundwater Contamination in The Navajo Nation. Geological Society of America 2024 annual meeting. Anaheim, CA (September 22-25, 2024)

Tibbits, D., *****Bebo, C.**, Chang, C., Witkowski, R., Prabhakar, L., Danyi, C., Pinnella, M., Olsen, P., RoyChowdhury, A., Kinney, S. An ICP-MS Calibrated XRF Geochemical Inventory of The Colorado Plateau Coring Project. Geological Society of America 2024 annual meeting. Anaheim, CA (September 22-25, 2024)

*Yazzie, T., Frey, B., Cadol, D., Tsosie, R., Sturgis, L., Woolsey, E., **RoyChowdhury, A**. Determining Key Factors in Well Selection Criteria for Navajo Technical University-New Mexico Tech-Navajo Nation Water Purification Project (N4WPP). New Mexico Geological Society (NMGS) Annual Spring Meeting, Socorro, NM (April 19, 2024)

*Yazzie, T., Frey, B., Tsosie, R., Cadol, D., Sturgis, L., **RoyChowdhury, A.**, *Wilson, D., Prush, V., Bowman, C. Developing a Selection Criteria to Install Water Filtration Units on the Navajo Reservation to Increase Water Supply. 2024 American Indian Science and Engineering Society (AISES) National Conference. San Antonio, TX (October 3-5, 2024)

Book Chapters

Biswas, P.K., Maughan, M.R., Kumar, A., **Singla, Y.K.** (2024). Analyzing Fractures in Nanomaterial-Enhanced Carbon Fiber-Reinforced Polymer (CFRP) Composites. In: Kumar, A., Kumar Singla, Y., Maughan, M.R. (eds) Fracture Behavior of Nanocomposites and Reinforced Laminate Structures. Springer, Cham. https://doi.org/10.1007/978-3-031-68694-8_12

Heidari, M., Khashehchi, M., Thangavel, S., Rahmanivahid, P., Kumar, A., **Singla, Y.K.** (2024). Laminated Structures and Fracture Mechanics: A Comprehensive Study of Mode 1, Mode II, and Mixed Mode III Behavior. In: Kumar, A., Kumar Singla, Y., Maughan, M.R. (eds) Fracture Behavior of Nanocomposites and Reinforced Laminate Structures. Springer, Cham. https://doi.org/10.1007/978-3-031-68694-8_18

Khashehchi, M., Heidari, M., Thangavel, S., Rahmanivahid, P., Kumar, A., **Singla, Y.K.** (2024). Insights into Aerospace Structural Integrity: A Study on Fiber/Epoxy Composites Fracture. In: Kumar, A., Kumar Singla, Y., Maughan, M.R. (eds) Fracture Behavior of Nanocomposites and Reinforced Laminate Structures. Springer, Cham. https://doi.org/10.1007/978-3-031-68694-8_20

Kumar, A., **Singla, Y.K., Biswas, P.,** Heidari, M., Thangavel, S. (2024). Resurrection Structure: New Generation of Bio-Inspired Nanocomposites and Laminates. In: Kumar, A., Kumar Singla, Y., Maughan, M.R. (eds) Fracture Behavior of Nanocomposites and Reinforced Laminate Structures. Springer, Cham. https://doi.org/10.1007/978-3-031-68694-8_17

Panja, S., Pal, R., **RoyChowdhury, A.** (2024). "Chapter 4 – Accumulation and Detoxification of Aqueous Pollutants by Microbes/Enzymes." In Microbes and Enzymes for Water Treatment and Remediation (1st ed.). Eds. Ashok Kumar Nadda, Priya Banerjee, and Swati Sharma. CRC Press, Taylor and Francis Group. Pages 64–78. https://doi.org/10.1201/9781003517238

Singla, Y.K., Kumar, A., Maughan, M.R. (2024). Introduction to Mechanical and Fracture Behavior Characterization of Nanocomposites and Reinforced Laminated Structures. In: Kumar, A., Kumar Singla, Y., Maughan, M.R. (eds) Fracture Behavior of Nanocomposites and Reinforced Laminate Structures. Springer, Cham. https://doi.org/10.1007/978-3-031-68694-8_1

Conclusion

Developing the research strength of NTU is still a work in process, but what has been achieved by a small rural college located on a Native American nation that has faced generational poverty for nearly all its existence during the treaty era is impressive.

ABOUT
THE AUTHORS

Thomas (Tom) Davis became the Assistant to the President when he retired as the Provost of NTU. Before coming to NTU, he started his career with the Menominee County Community School, one of the first Indian controlled schools in the United States and later served as the first Director of Planning for the Menominee Restoration Committee as the Menominee Tribe was restored to reservation status. He served as the President of a software development firm, Synaptic Micro Solutions, after that, and then helped found College of the Menominee Nation where he served as the Vice President of Academic Affairs. He has been the President of two tribal colleges, Lac Courtes Oreilles Ojibwa Community College and Little Priest Tribal College, and served as the Acting President and Academic Dean of Fond du Lac Tribal and Community College. He is a published writer who has had one non-fiction book about Menominee sustainable forestry, an autobiography about his experiences growing up and becoming involved in the Menominee Community School, five novels, three books of poetry, and two epic poems published. He has won several literary awards, including the Edna Ferber Fiction Award and his two-year reign as the Poet Laureate of Door County along with his wife, the artist and poet Ethel Mortenson Davis.

Dale Morgan serves as the Communications Specialist at Navajo Technical University (NTU), a role that perfectly aligns with his passion for creative expression and innovative technology. Having initially pursued Creative Writing at the University of New Mexico - Gallup, Dale found his true calling at NTU, where he majored in Creative Writing and New Media. Hailing from the community of Smith Lake, NM, Dale's dedication is evident from his two summer internships with the Ke'yah Advanced Rural Manufacturing Alliance (KARMA), where he made significant strides by developing a dynamic website. Dale strongly believes in the transformative power of technology in education and understands the importance of staying current in our fast-paced world. His involvement with KARMA has been impactful, notably participating in their 3D Printing Summer Camp alongside St. Bonaventure School and other local institutions. By advancing his skills; he's actively contributing to NTU's mission of fostering economic development and uplifting needy communities.

H Scott Halliday is currently the Coordinator of the Center for Advanced Manufacturing. Mr. Halliday started his career at NTU as a permanent substitute during the spring semester of 2003 in Computer Aided Drafting. Mr. Halliday was then hired in the Fall of 2003 to be the program director of the Computer Aided Drafting Certificate program. He then created an Associate's Degree program in Computer-Aided Drafting that combined classroom work with experiential projects that combined learning with doing. Mr. Halliday started facilitating student internships at Marshall Space Flight Center in Huntsville, Alabama in 2006 which led to the development of a 4-year Digital Manufacturing Degree with three concentrations; Digital Manufacturing, IT, and New Media, which ultimately led to the Engineering Programs in place at NTU today. Mr. Halliday then started to develop the Center for Advanced Manufacturing to provide students and faculty a means to not only apply their engineering concepts but to also engage in high level research concentrating in Metal Additive Manufacturing. Mr. Halliday and students have been co-authors on several metal AM publications.

Sheena Begay is the Director of Institutional Data and Reporting at Navajo Technical University. She embarked on a transformative educational journey as a first-generation college student, initially attending the College of Eastern Utah in Blanding, Utah and then at the University of Arizona in Tucson, Arizona before enrolling at Crownpoint Institute of Technology (CIT) in Crownpoint, New Mexico. Hailing from a rural part of the Navajo Nation, Sheena experienced firsthand the challenges of remote living, which instilled in her a deep appreciation for even the smallest conveniences. She played a pivotal role in CIT's transition to Navajo Technical College, serving as a member of numerous student clubs and as the Student Senate President and a Board member. Sheena has made significant contributions to the institution, including selecting Navajo Technical University's school mascot, the Skyhawks. After starting her professional role at NTU, she pursued a bachelor's degree in Sociology at the University of New Mexico in Albuquerque, New Mexico and later earned a master's in Management Information Systems from NTU.

Jared Ribble is a distinguished IT leader and the Director of Information Technology at Navajo Technical University.

A member of the Navajo Nation, he was born in Borrego Pass, NM and raised in the Little Water Chapter House community. After graduating from Crownpoint High School, he initially pursued pre-med studies at the University of New Mexico but later transitioned to the University of New Mexico Gallup branch due to cultural differences in large classroom settings.

His career path shifted when he enrolled at Crownpoint Institute of Technology (now NTU) and discovered a passion for IT through a programming course. He earned an associate degree in IT and became the institution's first IT technician. Over the past 23 years, he has built his career guided by mentors such as Chris Kearns and Tom Davis. He holds a Bachelor of Science in Information Technology from Salish Kootenai College and an earned master's degree from NTU.

Jared is currently designing the hardware, protocols, and routing for a missing and murdered relatives database, integrating AI and machine learning. He is also involved in rebuilding community wireless networks and recently completed an NSF Science DMZ project, improving campus network infrastructure and tribal connectivity at Diné College and Tohono O'odham Community College in Arizona. Additionally, he is finalizing the design for eduroam installation at NTU, expanding connectivity to local Chapter House networks and TCUs. His expertise spans IT infrastructure, networking, open-source technologies, and cluster building. Looking ahead, he plans to enhance the university's Science DMZ infrastructure with white box switching solutions, further strengthening tribal network capabilities.

Al Kuslikis has been involved in the Tribal College Movement since 1986, when he first began working at the

Shiprock campus of Navajo Community College (now Diné College) while conducting doctoral research in cognitive anthropology. His work at AIHEC spanned almost 20 years, during which time he focused on facilitating partnerships and developing projects that furthered the missions of both AIHEC and the TCU membership. Project areas included STEM education, economic development, cyberinfrastructure, climate resilience and health. Since retiring in 2023, Mr. Kuslikis has continued working on Tribal and TCU-relevant projects, including Indigenous digital humanities, STEM education, climate resilience and most recently, artificial intelligence.

Dr. Thiagarajan Soundappan is an Associate Professor in the Department of Chemistry at Navajo Technical University (NTU), where he also holds the roles of Chemistry Program Coordinator and Department Head. He brings over 15 years of experience in teaching and research, with specialized expertise in electrochemistry and advanced sensor development. His research portfolio encompasses the fabrication of electrochemical sensors, biosensors, and wearable devices. Dr. Soundappan's interests also extend to energy storage and conversion technologies, including redox flow batteries, lithium-ion batteries, fuel cells, and solar cells. At NTU, Dr. Soundappan leads the National Science Foundation (NSF) Partnerships for Research and Education in Materials (PREM) program as its Project Director, fostering collaborative research opportunities and advancing materials research capacity at the institution. Before joining NTU, Dr. Soundappan held prestigious postdoctoral positions in the Department of Chemistry at the University of Texas at Austin and at Washington University in St. Louis. His postdoctoral career was further distinguished by his selection for the Fondazione Oronzio e

Niccolò De Nora Postdoctoral and Dow Chemical Industrial Postdoctoral fellowships. Dr. Soundappan maintains active professional memberships in the Electrochemical Society (ECS), the American Chemical Society (ACS), and the Materials Research Society (MRS). He is a Sensor Division Session Chair for multiple ECS conferences, contributing to the global electrochemical research community. His scholarly output includes 43 peer-reviewed research publications and an edited book, reflecting his sustained contributions to the fields of chemistry, electrochemistry, and materials science.

Notes

---

[1] Drawn from Wikipedia

[2] From a text by Peter McDonald to Elmer Guy, 2/17/2005.

[3] The Indian Controlled Schools movement is significant in the history of American Indian education. Navajo had two important schools that played a role in the movement, the Rough Rock Demonstration School and Ramah Navajo High School. Eventually the Indian Controlled Schools movement schools became Bureau of Indian Affairs contract schools.

[4] Most of the early TCUs were started with short-term grants from private foundations. The first funding that helped move the schools beyond limited funding was provided by the U.S. Department of Education and the Title III, Strengthening Institutions program. The funding was only provided through partnerships with mainstream community colleges or colleges, but it did provide stability until eventually long-term legislation could be achieved.

[5] ABET accreditation is recognized as the gold standard accreditation for engineering and technical degrees worldwide.

[6] In the Western part of New Mexico, part of the Navajo Nation was checkerboarded because of the Dawes Act of 1887. The Dawes Act allotted land to individual Navajo households. Allotted lands were owned by those individual families. Some land not allotted were sold to non-Indian landowners, and some parcels were sold by the families that owned them, creating a checkerboarded pattern of private and tribal land.

[7] Guy, Elmer. 2018. "History of American Indian Vocational Rehabilitation Programs," PowerPoint presentation.

[8] This is the longest that any Navajo Chairman or President has served in that position during history.

[9] TCUs in the United States are funded in different ways. There are the schools funded primarily by the Tribally Controlled Community Colleges and Universities Act. Haskell Nations

University and Southwest Indian Polytechnic Institute are funded completely by the BIA and are considered federal colleges. The Institute of American Indian Arts was created by federal legislation. The Board of IAIA is appointed by the serving President of the United States. Navajo Community College was also created by federal legislation sponsored by the Navajo Nation, the Navajo Community College Act of 1971 and is funded by appropriations through that act. Today NCC is Diné College. Two colleges, United Tribes Community College, located in North Dakota, and NTU are primarily funded by the Carl D. Perkins Career and Technical Education Act and funds from the BIA originally dedicated to tribal economic development through career education. United Tribes and NTU, when the BIA funds were threatened, joined together to encourage passage of legislation that protected the funding.

[10] The 1862 Morrill Act created the land grant system. It dedicated rents from federal land in states to create state universities throughout the United States. The subsequent 1890 act required states to either integrate Black students into existing land-grant institutions or establish separate land-grant institutions for them, leading to the creation of many of the Historically Black Colleges and Universities (HBCUs) in existence today. The lands dedicated to creating the 1862 land grant universities came from what were once American Indian lands.

[11] Navajo Community College first achieved its accreditation in 1979, but the other colleges worked for several years after that to achieve accreditation.

[12] Ambler, Marjane. "Tribal Colleges Helped Shape Kellogg Agenda for Major Initiative," *Tribal College, Journal of American Indian Higher Education,* February 4, 1997, Vol 8, No. 4, accessed online at https://tribalcollegejournal.org/tribal-colleges-helped-shape-kellogg-agenda-major-initiative, 2/24/25.

[13] NCA is the North Central Accreditation agency that became the Higher Learning Commission, which is the current

federally accreditation agency for the Midwest part of the United States.

[14] This was changed from SMET to STEM (Science, Technology, Engineering, and Math) a couple of years later by NSF.

[15] Davis, Thomas. 2020. "How Not to Fall Off a Stage During Commencement," *Meditations on Ceremonies of Beginning*. Durango, CO: Tribal College Press, pp. 92-95.

[16] Hozein, Wafa.1/23/2023. "Building a Sustainable Water Infrastructure. *Native Science Report*. Accessed online at https://nativesciencereport.org/2023/06/building-a-sustainable-water-infrastructure, *3/18/25*.

[17] The current President and Vice President of the Navajo Nation.

[18] The current President and Vice President of the Navajo Nation.

[19] Carrie Billy was at that time the Director of the White House Office on Tribal Colleges and Universities under President William Clinton and recruited Kathy Isaacson and Stephen Littlejohn to lead the Circle of Prosperity, providing much of the funding for the event out of her office.

[20] The technology train metaphor used here was taken from a speech Tom Davis gave at the tribal prosperity game in 2000.

[21] An example of what is happening in China is the technology giant Hauawei's massive new technology center. The center consists of 104 individually designed buildings, labs for 35,000 scientists, engineers, and other workers, and perks designed to attract the best Chinese and foreign technologists and scientists. China yearly is graduating more engineers and scientists than there are total higher education student populations in the U.S.

[22] The University of Kansas School of Medicine (KUSM) in Salina, Kansas is a medical school that focuses on rural health. The school was established in 2011 to address the shortage of physicians in rural areas. This is the smallest medical school in the United States but has still been graduating increasingly larger classes of students.

[23] Jones, David S., "The persistence of American Indian health disparities," Am J Public Health doi: 10.2105/AJPH.2004.054262. Epub 2006 Oct 31. 2006.

[24] This occurred during a meeting in Window Rock at the Vice President's office between representatives of NTU, Diné College, Vice President Rex Lee Jim, and his staff in 2012.

[25] Senate Committee on Indian Affairs. Retrieved 10/9/13.

[26] Rivo, Marc L. and Kindig, David A. N Engl J Med 1996; 334:892-896. April 4, 1996, DOI: 10.1056/NEJM199604043341405.

[27] Ibid.

[28] ChatGPT search conducted on 2/27/25.

[29] NTU offers a Certified Nurse Assistant program and an associate degree in Registered Nursing (RN) currently.

www.ingramcontent.com/pod-product-compliance
Lightning Source LLC
Chambersburg PA
CBHW071157210326
41597CB00016B/1577